THE
VOYAGES OF
CAPTAIN
COOK

THE VOYAGES OF
CAPTAIN COOK

REX and THEA RIENITS

PAUL HAMLYN

LONDON·NEW YORK·SYDNEY·TORONTO

AUTHOR'S NOTE

Dates throughout the voyages are as they appear in Cook's journals—from noon to noon while at sea, and from midnight to midnight during long periods ashore. For ease of reading the spelling and punctuation of quotations from journals and other documents have been brought into line with modern usage. Likewise, names of native places and people have been given their modern rendering. Thus, for instance, Otaheite has become Tahiti, and Oberea has become Purea.

Half-title page Thousands of Londoners and tourists know this statue of Cook, which stands in The Mall near Admiralty Arch. The sculptor was Sir T. Brock, RA, and it was erected in 1914

Frontispiece Engraved portrait of Cook, after Webber

Published by
THE HAMLYN PUBLISHING GROUP LTD
LONDON · NEW YORK · SYDNEY · TORONTO
Hamlyn House, The Centre, Feltham, Middlesex
© Copyright 1968 the Hamlyn Publishing Group Ltd
Phototypeset by
BAS Printers Limited, Wallop, Hampshire
Printed in Hong Kong by
Toppan Printing Company (H.K.) Limited

CONTENTS

Whitby harbour as Cook knew it in
the mid-18th century. Water-colour
by an unknown artist

PRELUDE

It is said that George III wept when he learned of the death of James Cook. If so he did not weep alone, for all Britain mourned and not only Britain but her friends and her enemies and the whole western world. No one could be sure how the people of his favourite island, Tahiti, would have reacted, for in their eyes he was a demi-god and presumably immortal, and it was not thought prudent to disillusion them.

Cook was essentially a man of peace. He never commanded a ship of the line and he never fought in a major naval engagement; yet apart from Nelson he remains today the most famous of all Britain's captains, and this surely is the measure of his greatness. He was a natural leader of men, a peerless seaman and navigator, a superb cartographer, an acute and accurate observer, and the foremost explorer of his own or any age. He died knowing that his achievements in three historic voyages made between 1768 and 1779 could never be surpassed or even again be equalled for he had left comparatively little for others to do.

It is almost impossible to overstate the extent of Cook's contribution to geographical knowledge. On the negative side he silenced forever those theorists—among them his implacable detractor Alexander Dalrymple—who insisted there must be a great southern continent to counterbalance the land mass of the northern hemisphere, and he disproved the theory that there existed a practical north-west passage around the top of America (although sixty years were to pass and men like Sir John Franklin were to die before his word was finally accepted). On the positive side he discovered and charted much of the Pacific that we know today from the west coast of Canada and the Hawaiian islands to New Caledonia; he established, by sailing around it, that New Zealand was no part of a mythical continent but two large, narrowly-separated islands; he disproved the Dutch belief that New Holland was entirely barren by traversing the whole length of its fertile eastern coast, thus paving the way for British settlement there eighteen years later; and he confirmed that a strait separated New Guinea from what is now Australia.

He did much more, however. He pioneered and perfected the use of the chronometer to determine longitude, and so took a lot of the guess-work out of navigation. He showed by practical example how scurvy, the greatest single scourge of seafarers, could be controlled and conquered. He wrote simply and informatively about the places he visited and with humanity and insight about the people he met and how they lived. His accounts of his voyages, illustrated by the various artists who accompanied him, became best-selling books which not only broadened the knowledge and mental horizons of the many who read them but lent such apparent weight to the theories of Rousseau and other philosophers of the back-to-nature school that it took several decades of earnest missionary propaganda to tarnish the popular image of the 'noble savage'. And as father of modern marine surveying he established a tradition and founded a line which extended through Vancouver, Bligh, Broughton, Flinders, Owen, FitzRoy and many others far into the nineteenth century.

The attic room in Grape Lane,
Whitby, in which Cook studied
mathematics and navigation as an
apprentice. Etching by
L. T. Crawshaw, RA

It is remarkable enough that any one man could have achieved so much, but in Cook's case it is even more remarkable that he was ever given the chance to do so, for he came into the world with no advantage at all save his own intelligence and will. His parents were poor, he had no influential relatives or friends, he had to work for a living when more fortunate children were still at school. Even today such handicaps can be formidable. In the age of privilege into which he was born they were almost insurmountable until Cook himself proved otherwise.

He was born on 27th October 1728 at Marton, a small village south of Middlesbrough in the Cleveland district of Yorkshire, the second of seven children of James and Grace Cook. His father, a farm-labourer, was a Scot, his mother a local girl. Not enough is known of his parents to indicate from which side he inherited his genius; indeed, during his formative years there was

little to suggest that such a quality existed. During his infancy the family moved to Great Ayton, a larger village where there was a school, and when he was old enough his father's employer paid for him to attend this. Although he absorbed all it had to offer his education was brief and elementary. His late boyhood was spent working with his father on the farm, and there but for his driving ambition he may well have remained. Instead, however, at the age of seventeen he took his first step towards emancipation when he became apprenticed to a grocer and haberdasher in the fishing village of Staithes. His employer was a kindly man, but young Cook soon realised he was not cut out for trade, and once the tang of salt was fairly in his nostrils he had no doubt where his future lay. After eighteen months, at his own insistent request, his indentures were cancelled, and in July 1746 with his master's help he was apprenticed to John and Henry Walker, shipowning

A muster-roll for 1752–53 of the
Whitby collier *Friendship*, on which
Cook served as mate. His name is
second on the list

brothers of the nearby port of Whitby.

Cook's first taste of life at sea was aboard the *Freelove*, a collier trading between Newcastle and London, and he stayed in her two years. Between voyages and during the winters when she was laid up he lived with his employers, and with their encouragement he spent long hours studying mathematics and navigation and filling in the gaps in his general education. In the next few years there were voyages in various ships to Ireland and the Baltic. All the time as he served before the mast Cook was absorbing and learning, coming to terms not only with the sea and with ships, but with his fellow-men. He was too earnest and single-minded, too silent and remote to make friends easily, but in place of friendship he won the respect and admiration of those he worked with. When his time was up he left the Walkers for a while, but in 1752 at the age of twenty-three he rejoined them as mate of the *Friendship*, another of

their colliers on the coastal run. Less than three years later he was offered the command of the same ship and his future seemed assured. But instead he turned it down, and on 17th June 1755 he enlisted in the British Navy as an ordinary seaman.

Cook's decision was not so surprising, really. In theory Europe was at peace; in fact most of the major Powers, and particularly Britain and France, were arming intensively for what was to become the Seven Years' War, and as a prelude to this British ships were already blockading the French coast to hamper the reinforcement of the French colonies. New ships were coming off the slipways as fast as they could be built, and to man them press-gangs were combing every seaport in England. Cook had no need to worry on this score for as the master of a merchantman he would have been immune from forcible enlistment. But this was not the point. In peacetime naval promotion was slow and depended largely on patronage; in wartime it was quick and depended primarily on ability. In peacetime it would have been presumptuous of a farm labourer's son to aspire to be a naval officer; in wartime it was not. Cook simply saw his opportunity and took it, though there is a strong presumption that patriotism played a part as well.

A week after he had enlisted Cook went aboard HMS *Eagle*, sixty guns, at Portsmouth as an AB. Within a month he was master's mate, and the career which was to raise him to the pinnacle of fame was under way. From the day he joined the *Eagle* he kept a log. Like himself it was laconic and to the point. It recorded alarms and chases and skirmishes. Strange sail were stopped and searched and occasional prizes were taken. Twice the *Eagle* in search of her prey ventured so close in to Cherbourg that she came under fire from the guns of the fort. It was all fairly routine and not particularly dramatic but for Cook it was an invaluable experience, for above all he was now learning the importance of discipline—the tough, hard naval discipline which, imposed impartially on others and on himself, was to make the difference between success and failure and at times even between life and death, in the years ahead.

Up to this point luck had played little part in Cook's career. Now it took a welcome hand. There was a change of command on the *Eagle*, and Cook found himself serving under Captain Hugh Palliser, an officer of outstanding ability and perception. In time Palliser was to become governor of Newfoundland and a Lord of the Admiralty, yet these things are almost forgotten and he is remembered today mainly as the man who first recognised and encouraged the genius of James Cook; indeed, in his later years this became Palliser's own proudest boast.

When Britain officially declared war on France early in 1756 Cook was still on the *Eagle*, and on her he remained for more than another year. Then she was badly damaged in an action in which she captured a French East Indiaman, the *Duc d'Aquitaine*, and when she was laid up for repairs Cook was transferred to another ship. He was due for promotion and his old Whitby friends, the Walkers, urged that he should be given a commission. But for all his good will Palliser was obliged to point out that his length of service did not yet entitle him to this. Instead, when he went aboard the *Pembroke*, sixty-four guns, on his twenty-ninth birthday, 27th October 1757, he did so with the warrant of master.

By the beginning of 1758 British armed strength was concentrated against the French in Canada, and during February the *Pembroke* was one of nineteen ships of the line which sailed for that theatre. The great objective was Quebec, but first the strongly defended fortress of Louisburg at the mouth of the Gulf of St Lawrence had to be reduced. The *Pembroke* was still at her base at

Above Title page of navigational note book by Archibald Hamilton, 1763, showing on the right a navigator with his log, compass and octant

Top right Sir Hugh Palliser, who as captain of HMS *Eagle* was the first man to recognize Cook's genius. Portrait attributed to George Dance

Bottom right A mariner's compass of the mid-18th century, made by Adams

Halifax when the first bloody frontal assault was launched, but she was active in the siege that followed and was present when the battered French garrison lowered their colours after seven weeks on 26th July.

The way to Quebec was now open, but British casualties had been high. Reinforcements were needed and damaged ships had to be repaired, and these things took time. Winter clamped down and the St Lawrence River iced over and even when the spring thaw came much still remained to be done. In particular there remained the task of finding a safe channel up the St Lawrence. As it approaches Quebec the river narrows and is studded with shoals, rocks and reefs. The French had removed all buoys and other navigation marks, and although charts of the river had been captured it was necessary to check these and amend them where necessary. The task was entrusted to the masters of several ships, among them Cook. It was slow and exacting work, and within range of the French artillery it became extremely hazardous as well. For weeks, working often at night, Cook and his colleagues carried on quietly and painstakingly in constant danger of death or capture. At last every inch of the river had been resurveyed, resounded and recharted and a safe channel marked. During June more than two hundred warships and transports sailed up this channel without a single casualty to anchor in the basin before Quebec, and the siege of the city had begun. Almost three months later on the night of 12th September British troops under Wolfe stormed the Heights of Abraham, and when it was over Quebec had fallen and both Wolfe and the French defender, Montcalm, were dead.

Many of the British warships including the *Pembroke* were sent home for refit. But Cook stayed on, transferred to the *Northumberland*, the flagship of Admiral Lord Colville, commander-in-chief of the North American station. On Colville's personal order he continued to chart the St Lawrence, both east of Quebec and as far west as Montreal, and he did such a thorough job that he received a bonus of £50 'in consideration of his indefatigable industry in making himself master of the pilotage of the river'. Through most of 1762 he surveyed and charted a considerable part of the coast of the island of Newfoundland. Colville sent home for publication his meticulously-drawn charts with a note to the Admiralty urging that Cook should be employed 'on greater undertakings of the same kind', and warmly commending his 'genius'. It was the first time the word had been applied to him in official correspondence; it was certainly not to be the last.

The war was almost over when the *Northumberland* returned to England towards the end of 1762. Cook was paid off and went ashore with the tidy sum of £291 to his credit. Six weeks later, on 21st December, at St Margaret's, Barking, he married Elizabeth Batts. He was thirty-four, his bride twenty-one. They may have

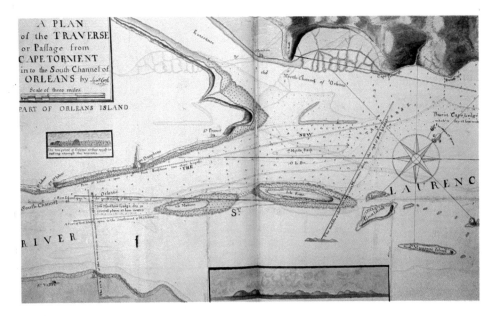

Left Captain James Cook, by John Webber. This picture was painted at Cook's request early in 1776 before he set out on his third voyage, as a present for his wife. It is now in the National Art Gallery, Wellington, New Zealand

Above Cook's plan of The Traverse in the St Lawrence River, near Quebec. By following this more than 200 British warships sailed up the river without casualty and began the siege of the city

Right Whitby's own tribute to Cook is this bronze statue by John Tweed

Below Navigational instruments were greatly improved during the latter half of the 18th century. This sextant, by an unknown maker, is of the type which Cook probably used during his survey of the coasts of Newfoundland and Labrador

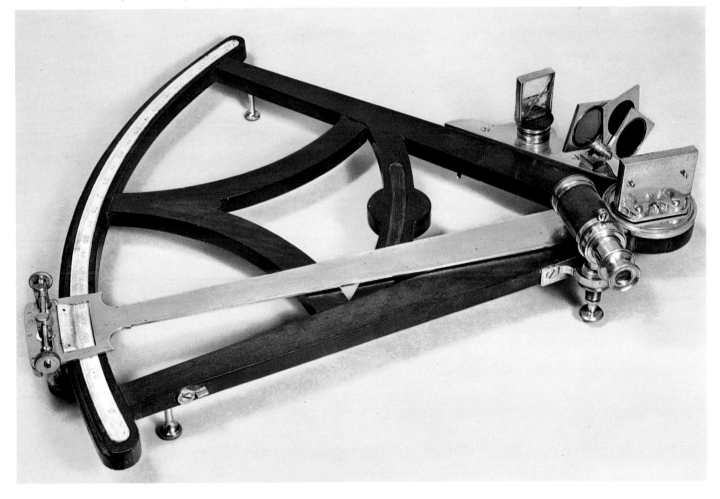

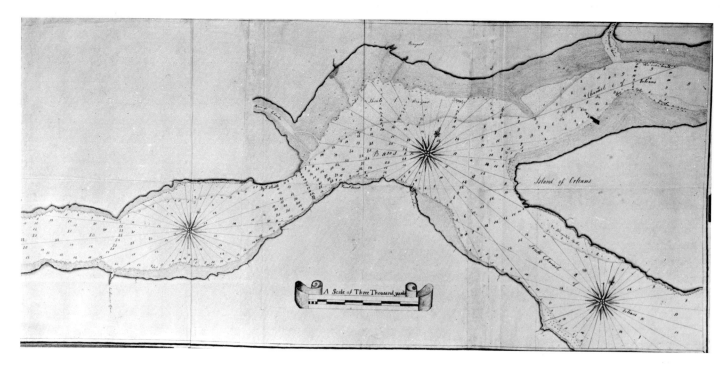

Above Cook's chart of the Quebec basin on the St Lawrence River

Top right Cook's plan of York Harbour, Labrador, which he surveyed in 1762, was one of many which established his reputation as the Navy's best cartographer

Bottom right. A record of Cook's voyages as a merchant seaman, compiled from muster rolls

known each other before he had left England but this is uncertain. Even if they had she would have been little more than a girl at the time, so in either case it was a remarkably quick wooing for a man usually so unimpulsive as Cook. They took a small house in Shadwell, in the east end of London, but their time together was short. In April Cook was recalled to duty specifically to continue his survey of the Newfoundland coast, and in the same month he sailed in HMS *Antelope*.

In the next five years his life followed a fairly regular pattern. His summers were spent around Newfoundland or on the coast of Labrador, and his winters in England completing the charts he had made. These were published in the *North American Pilot* and they were so accurate and so complete that they were not superseded for more than a century. On his first return to London late in 1763 Cook found he was the father of a six-weeks-old son, James. He and his wife moved to a house in Mile End Row which was to be their home during the rest of his life and remained Mrs Cook's for several years of her widowhood.

When Cook reached Newfoundland for the following summer's work his old commander, Captain Palliser,

was already installed as governor of the province. Palliser knew Cook's quality as perhaps no other man did, and on his recommendation Cook was given his own ship, the *Grenville*, a small schooner well adapted for survey work. It was his first command after nine years in the Navy, but he still remained uncommissioned. His long and exacting task continued until 1767, and in the autumn he left eastern Canada for what was to be the last time. In the years between there had been two further additions to his family—Nathaniel, born in 1764, and Elizabeth in 1766.

The farm boy had come a long way. Although still only a warrant officer, his reputation as a cartographer and navigator was second to none, and he had proved himself also a zealous and able commander. His detailed report of an eclipse of the sun which he had observed off Newfoundland in 1766 had been published by the Royal Society, and this had brought him also to the notice of men of science. In his fortieth year, at a time of life when many naval officers were already past their peak, he was obviously poised on the threshhold of a notable career. But no one, least of all Cook himself, could guess how great that career was to be.

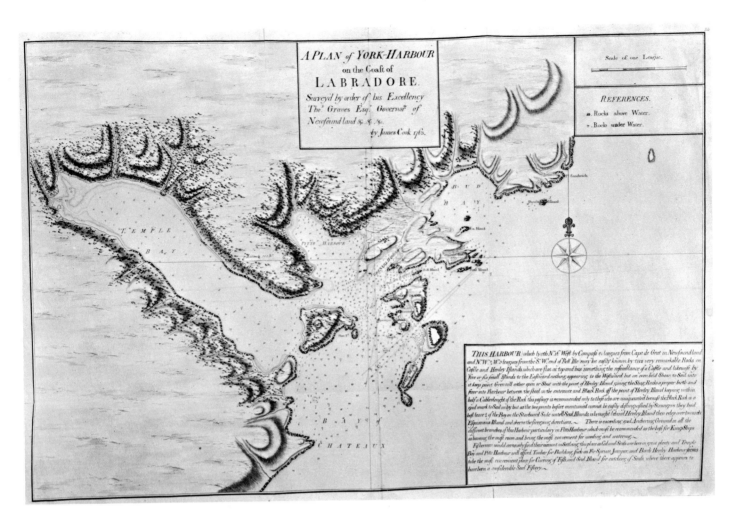

JAMES COOK IN WHITBY SHIPS

FROM THE OLD SAILORS INSURANCE BOOKS ENTITLED "THE MUSTER ROLLS" AND KEPT AT THE SEAMEN'S HOSPITAL, CHURCH STREET, WHITBY.

ENTRIES SHOWING JAMES COOK'S NAME ON THE ROLL.

SHIP	CAPTAIN OF SHIP	OWNER	AGE	RATING	DOMICILE OR PLACE OF BIRTH	DATES OF ENTRY AND DISCHARGE, 1747-1755	LAST SHIP	NOTES
FREELOVE FULL RIGGER IN COAL TRADE	JOHN JEFFERSON	JOHN WALKER	19	SERVANT	MARTON, Gt. AYTON	29/9/47 - 14/12/47	FREELOVE	COOK'S PREVIOUS VOYAGE IS NOT FOUND IN THESE BOOKS
FREELOVE	JOHN JEFFERSON	JOHN WALKER	19	SERVANT	WHITBY	26/2/48 - 7/6/48	FREELOVE	
THREE BROTHERS	JOHN WALKER AND JOHN JEFFERSON	JOHN WALKER		SERVANT	WHITBY	14/7/48 - 14/10/48	FREELOVE	THE SHIP WAS TAKEN TO LONDON BY JOHN WALKER AND WAS FITTED AS A TRANSPORT WITH 40 STALLS FOR HORSES
THREE BROTHERS	JOHN WALKER AND JOHN JEFFERSON	JOHN WALKER	20	SERVANT	WHITBY	14/10/48 - 20/4/49	THREE BROTHERS	PRESUMABLY STILL IN TRANSPORT SERVICE
THREE BROTHERS	JOHN JEFFERSON	JOHN WALKER		SEAMAN	ATON	20/4/49 - 26/9/49	THREE BROTHERS	IN NORWEGIAN SERVICE
THREE BROTHERS	JOHN JEFFERSON	JOHN WALKER		SEAMAN	ATON	27/9/49 - 8/12/49	THREE BROTHERS	
MARY	WILLIAM GASKIN			SEAMAN	WHITBY	8/2/50 - 5/10/50		LAST SHIP NOT GIVEN
THREE BROTHERS	ROBERT WATSON	JOHN WALKER		SEAMAN	YATTON	-/11/51 - -/11/52	THREE BROTHERS	THIS WAS COOK'S LAST VOYAGE IN THE THREE BROTHERS THERE IS A GAP BETWEEN THE MARY AND THIS VOYAGE
FRIENDSHIP	RICHARD ELLERTON	JOHN WALKER		MATE	AYTON	-/3/52 - -/11/52	THREE BROTHERS	COOK IS NOW MATE OF THE SHIP AND REMAINS WITH IT IN THAT POSE
FRIENDSHIP	JOHN SWAINSTON	JOHN WALKER		MATE	MARTON	2/2/53 - 4/2/54	FRIENDSHIP	
FRIENDSHIP	RICHARD ELLERTON	JOHN WALKER		MATE	MARTON	-/4/54 - -/7/54	FRIENDSHIP	
FRIENDSHIP	RICHARD ELLERTON	JOHN WALKER		MATE	MARTON	-/8/54 - -/12/54	FRIENDSHIP	
FRIENDSHIP	RICHARD ELLERTON	JOHN WALKER		MATE	YATTON	-/2/55 - 14/7/55	FRIENDSHIP	COOK WAS ASKED TO COMMAND THE SHIP AFTER THIS VOYAGE BUT PREFERRED TO JOIN THE NAVY AT A LOWER RATING

Thomas Luny's painting, now in the
National Library, Canberra, of the
collier *Earl of Pembroke* leaving
Whitby Harbour. Soon afterwards she
was to become famous as the
Endeavour

THE FIRST
VOYAGE
1768-1771

Among scientists it was known that on 3rd June 1769 the planet Venus would pass between the earth and the sun, a phenomenon which would not occur again for more than a century. Accurate observation of this transit, as it was called, would add greatly to astronomical knowledge, on which navigation so much depended, and in particular it would help towards calculating the earth's distance from the sun. The Royal Society, which boasted that as astronomers the British were 'inferior to no nation on earth, ancient or modern', felt strongly that something should be done. A committee recommended that the transit should be observed from three points—the North Cape, at the Arctic tip of Scandinavia; Fort Churchill, in Hudson's Bay, Canada; and a suitable island in the South Pacific, perhaps one of the Marquesas or Tongan groups—and that two competent observers should be sent to each. The project was warmly approved by George III. He arranged for the Navy to provide ships, and on his order £4000 was granted to the Society to defray expenses.

Alexander Dalrymple, a geographer of some note who had had practical seagoing experience as commander of an East India merchantman, was recommended by the Society to head the South Seas mission. Dalrymple was willing but insisted that he would accept the appointment only if he were given command of the ship. This demand brought a predictable reaction from Sir Edward Hawke, First Lord of the Admiralty, who thumped the table and declared that he would sooner lose his right hand than give the command of a King's ship to a man who had not been bred to the Navy. Dalrymple refused to compromise, and the Society had to think again.

The obvious man, the one man who qualified in every possible regard, was of course James Cook. It is probable that he was recommended by Palliser, and he must have been approached as early as March 1768, for it can hardly be a coincidence that the ship which the Navy chose and bought during that month for the voyage was the *Earl of Pembroke*, a Whitby-built bark of three hundred and sixty-eight tons, round-bowed and deep-waisted, a slowish sailer but solidly reliable, of the type Cook had known so well during his years in the coal trade. She was renamed *Endeavour* (or more accurately *The Endeavour Bark*) and early in April she was transferred to Deptford to be sheathed, armed and otherwise fitted for the long voyage. Cook's appointment was officially announced at the beginning of May. On the 25th he was commissioned first lieutenant, and two days later he hoisted his pendant aboard the *Endeavour*. It must have been a proud moment. As his co-observer the Society appointed Charles Green, an able young astronomer, a Yorkshireman like Cook himself, the son of a farmer. Each was to receive a victualling allowance of £120 a year, with a gratuity at the end of the voyage.

There was still some vagueness as to the *Endeavour*'s destination. The Marquesas Islands had not been seen since their discovery by Mendaña in 1595 and the Tongan group since their discovery by Tasman in 1643. They were specks in a vast ocean, their precise whereabouts in doubt, and Cook would virtually have to rediscover whichever was chosen. Whether he could do so and still arrive in time to observe the transit was debatable. However, the problem solved itself with the return to England on 20th May of HMS *Dolphin* from a round-the-world voyage of almost two years. She had failed in her main mission—to find a continent in the southern hemisphere—but she had discovered an island in the Pacific which her commander, Samuel Wallis, had named after his sovereign and which its native inhabitants called Tahiti. It was a large island with several excellent anchorages. Food, water and wood were plentiful, and the Tahitians were friendly, gentle and attractive. Moreover, its location was so precisely known that any competent navigator could find it without trouble.

The Society recommended to the Admiralty that Tahiti should be Cook's destination. At the same time it sought permission for one of its Fellows, Joseph Banks, to join the expedition with a suite of seven assistants and servants. Both requests were granted. Banks was described accurately as 'a gentleman of large fortune, who is well versed in natural history'. His family seat was Revesby Abbey, Lincolnshire, and he had been its master since coming of age four years ago. He had been educated at Harrow, Eton and Christ Church, Oxford, but natural history rather than the classics had always been his passion. In 1766 he had gone on a plant-hunting expedition to Newfoundland, and the success of this had established him as a botanist of great promise. His two ambitions were to travel the world and to achieve fame as a naturalist, and here was a unique opportunity to realise both. He had influential friends to support his request, and he was able and willing to pay. The voyage is said to have cost him £10,000.

There is no record that Cook resented having eight extra people—in the event it turned out to be nine—foisted on him. The contrast between these two men who were to spend almost three years in the enforced intimacy

Joseph Banks, by Joshua Reynolds. It is thought to have been painted soon after his return from Cook's first voyage, and was exhibited at the Royal Academy in 1773

of shipboard life could hardly have been greater. For a start, there was a gap of fourteen years between them. Banks had enjoyed every advantage in life that Cook had lacked—wealthy parents, a sheltered upbringing, a thorough education, friends in high places. Circumstances apart, there were wide differences in their temperaments. Banks was extrovert, gay, charming, gregarious; Cook was a man used to solitude—self-contained, silent and even a little dour. Yet they also had much in common. To the extent that natural history was Banks's obsessive interest he was equally as self-taught as Cook. Both were positive, strongly individual characters; both were ambitious, and both were dedicated—Banks the gifted amateur, Cook the solid professional. Banks had the authority of his birth and breeding, Cook the disciplined authority of his experience. Both were men of high intelligence, and as events were to prove each had the humility to learn from the other. It is not surprising that they finished the voyage as close friends, nor that in later years Banks spoke of Cook as the greatest man he had ever known.

Banks's suite on the *Endeavour* comprised Dr Daniel Carl Solander, Herman Didrich Spöring, Francis Parkinson, Alexander Buchan and four servants. Solander, who travelled as a friend rather than as an employee, was a Swede of thirty-five, a short, rotund merry fellow liked by all. He had studied medicine at Uppsala University but had forsaken it for botany and had become one of the most brilliant pupils of the great Linneaus. As a Fellow of the Royal Society and a specialist on the staff of the British Museum he was generally conceded to be the ablest botanist in England. Spöring was also a Swede, a son of the professor of medicine at the University of Åbo (now Turku, Finland). Like Solander he had given up medicine for natural history and, seeking his fortune in England, had eventually earned a solid reputation in his chosen sphere.

A scale model of Cook's ship *Endeavour*, now in the National Maritime Museum, Greenwich

Among other things he was also a good draughtsman. Parkinson was twenty-three, the younger of two sons of Joel Parkinson, a Quaker brewer of Edinburgh. He had been apprenticed to a wool-draper, but his inclination was strongly towards natural history drawing, in which he had early gained a local reputation. In 1767 he had come to London, where Banks had employed him to make water-colour drawings of birds and animals from specimens and sketches brought from abroad. Among Parkinson's personal attributes, according to his brother Stanfield, were 'his singular simplicity of conduct, his sincere regard for truth, his ardent thirst after knowledge, and his indefatigable industry to obtain it'. Even allowing for brotherly enthusiasm the description was accurate enough. Presumably Buchan was also a Scot, but nothing is known of him beyond Banks's own statement that he was 'an ingenious and good young man', skilled in landscape and figure painting. This was to be his province on the voyage, as

Parkinson's was to be the delineation of natural history specimens. It is to be noted that the *Endeavour* was the first ship ever to sail with such a full staff of scientists, and that the precedent thus set was to be followed very many times during the next century.

With his general instructions for the voyage Cook received from the Admiralty certain sealed 'secret' instructions. After observing the transit of Venus at Tahiti he was to sail south as far as latitude 40 to search for *Terra Australis Incognita*, the supposed southern continent. If he failed to find this he was to turn west until he fell in with New Zealand, which Tasman had discovered and partly examined a hundred and twenty-five years before, and which Dalrymple and others believed to be a promontory of the continent. Having explored the New Zealand coast he was free to make his own way home to England. These instructions remained so 'secret' that Banks was able to discuss them in detail at a dinner party in London on the eve of his departure

Dr Daniel Carl Solander, the Swedish naturalist, who sailed in the *Endeavour*

DR SOLANDER, F.R.S.

to join the ship; and three days later the London *Gazetteer* was able to inform its readers that Cook was 'to attempt some new discoveries in that vast unknown tract above the latitude 40.'

When the *Endeavour* sailed from Plymouth on 26th August 1768 she had on board seventy-one crew, twelve marines and eleven supernumeraries, a total of ninety-four. The return of the *Dolphin* had been fortunate for Cook in more ways than one, for many who had once tasted the delights of Tahiti were avid to do so again. From numerous volunteers he chose four men of solid worth and experience—John Gore (3rd lieutenant), Robert Molyneux (master), Richard Pickersgill (master's mate) and Francis Wilkinson, AB, who became a master's mate during the voyage. His second lieutenant was Zachary Hicks, aged twenty-nine, and his surgeon was William Monkhouse, whose young brother Jonathan sailed as a midshipman. The company also included Mrs Cook's cousin, Isaac Smith, aged sixteen, who

enrolled as an AB, became a midshipman during the voyage, and eventually rose to become a rear-admiral.

Madeira was reached on 13th September. During a stay of five days Banks and Solander botanized assiduously around Funchal, and the hundreds of specimens they collected kept Parkinson busy at his drawing-board during the next stage of the voyage. Fresh beef, fruit, vegetables, wine and water were taken aboard, and Cook, who had very positive ideas about combating scurvy, issued every man with twenty pounds of onions, with a firm order that they were to be eaten. A seaman and a marine who refused to eat fresh beef were flogged; and a master's mate who became entangled in an anchor rope was drowned.

The equator was crossed on 26th October, and those who could not prove they had been south of the line—including Cook—had either to pay a bottle of rum or be ducked in the sea. Between twenty and thirty took their ducking, but Banks and Solander and presumably Cook

Sydney Parkinson, Banks's natural history draughtsman aboard the *Endeavour*

SYDNEY PARKINSON

Left Artocarpis communis, the Tahitian breadfruit, called by the natives 'uru'. A water-colour drawing by Sydney Parkinson

Below The Bay of Good Success, Tierra del Fuego, with natives and huts. This is one of the few surviving paintings by Alexander Buchan, who died soon afterwards in Tahiti

Right A man of Tahiti in full mourning garb, by an unknown artist aboard the *Endeavour*

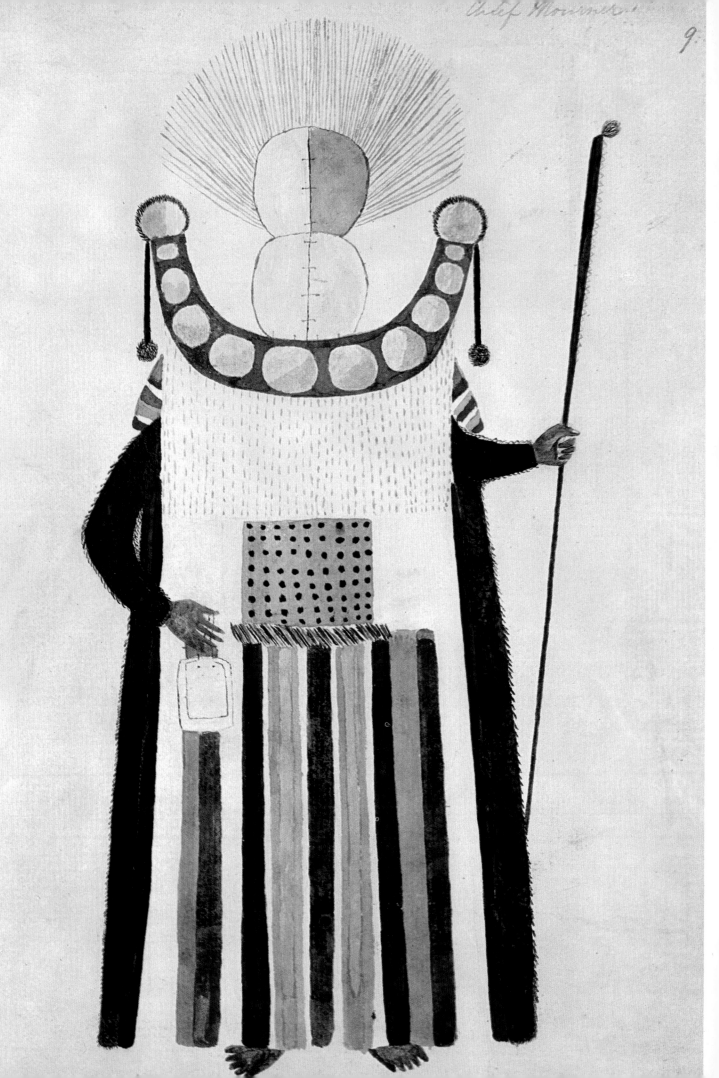

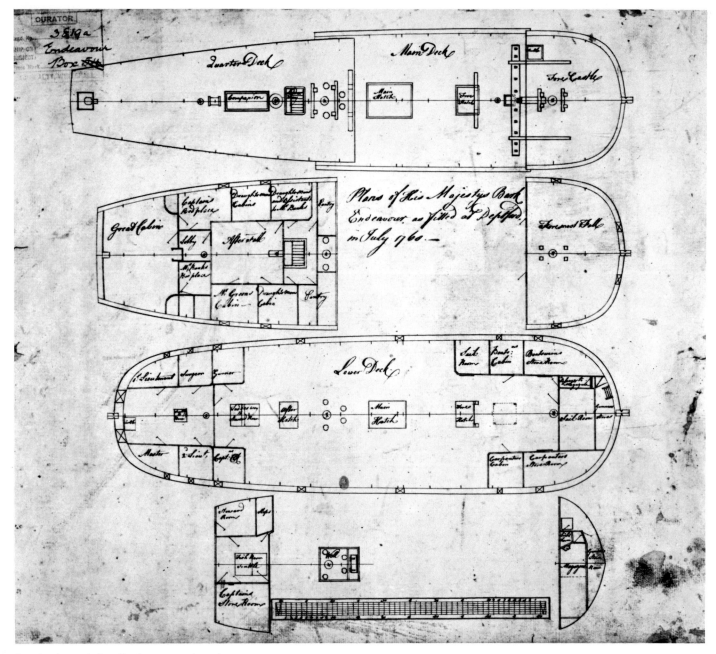

Deck plan of the *Endeavour,* showing
how cabin space was adjusted to
accommodate Banks and his suite

as well preferred to pay their forfeits.

At Rio de Janeiro, which was reached on 13th November, there was unexpected trouble with the Portuguese viceroy, who was new in his job and over-zealous. The *Endeavour* looked so unlike a warship that he found it hard to believe she was one, and it was beyond his credibility that a ship should sail round the world merely to make an astronomical observation. He convinced himself she was a smuggler, and gave orders accordingly. An armed guard was put on board, only Cook himself and those who could prove they were on duty were allowed ashore, and all supplies had to be bought through an agent. Cook protested and a paper war ensued. Banks helped by drafting Cook's memorials

and letters, and added some of his own. But the viceroy yielded not an inch, and on one occasion Hicks and some seamen who had been sent ashore on business were arrested and spent a night in the lock-up.

For Banks and his people the prohibition was particularly exasperating. Buchan made some excellent pencil sketches of Rio from the ship, but was unable to get close enough to draw any of the inhabitants. On two occasions Banks smuggled servants ashore at daybreak, and they returned at night bringing many exotic plants and insects. Thus encouraged Banks did the same, and Solander also managed to get ashore by pretending he was the ship's doctor and had been summoned to treat a patient in the town. But word of

A sketch from Parkinson's note-book
of the hull of the *Endeavour*

their exploit leaked out, and wisely they did not try again. When the *Endeavour* attempted to sail on 5th December she was fired on from the fort, and another two days passed before she was able to leave. Once she was clear of the harbour Banks persuaded Cook to anchor off a small island, and he and Solander went ashore and gathered plants to their hearts' content. In spite of everything they collected during their stay more than three hundred species, of which several were unknown to botanists in Europe.

'Yesterday being Christmas Day the people were none of the soberest,' Cook recorded laconically on 26th December. Banks was more explicit. 'All good Christians, that is to say all hands, got abominably

drunk,' he wrote, 'so that at night there was scarce a sober man in the ship. The wind, thank God, very moderate or the Lord knows what would have become of us.' As the *Endeavour* was more than three hundred miles from the nearest land his remark was not without point.

By 12th January 1769 the *Endeavour* was off the east coast of Tierra del Fuego, the bleak, wind-swept island at the southern tip of South America. For Banks's sake Cook looked for a suitable anchorage, and found one in what he called the Bay of Good Success. In four exciting hours ashore Banks and Solander found about a hundred plants quite new to them. Two days later Banks led a large party inland on another plant-hunting expedition.

An impression by an unknown artist
aboard the *Endeavour* of a Tahitian
long house, with coconut palms, a
breadfruit and other trees, and
natives in canoes. The two canoes
on left have fighting platforms, and a
mock battle appears to be in progress

It proved disastrous. Buchan had an epileptic fit and as a result the party were caught by nightfall in blizzardly weather. Solander went to sleep in the snow and had to be forcibly wakened and helped to a fire, and two of Banks's servants, both negroes, froze to death after having surreptitiously drunk most of the rum supply. The survivors returned to the ship next morning, and in spite of his exhaustion Banks spent the day fishing.

The natives were friendly enough, but to European eyes they were unattractive and uncouth. Cook described them as 'something above the middle size, of a dark copper colour, with long black hair', their only garment a cloak of raw llama or sealskin. 'The women wear a piece of skin over their private parts, but the men observe no such decency,' he added. Their huts were flimsy and open to the weather, and their only apparent diet was shellfish. Buchan tried to draw them but he was too unwell to produce more than a few stiff pencil sketches and water-colours. Parkinson also made some

sketches which he worked up into a large wash drawing.

The weather continued moderate as the *Endeavour* made her way through Le Maire Strait, and Cape Horn was rounded without difficulty on 24th January. During the whole passage, Cook wrote with satisfaction, it was never found necessary to close-reef the topsails, 'a circumstance that perhaps never happened before to any ship in these seas'.

The voyage north-west towards Tahiti was leisurely and pleasant, marred by only one unhappy incident. A young marine was caught in the act of stealing a piece of sealskin from which he meant to make a pouch, and when his sergeant threatened to report him to Cook he slipped quietly overboard, unseen. During the first days of April several low atolls on the eastern fringe of the Tuamotus were passed and named. On 11th April the peaks of Tahiti were visible, and on the 13th the *Endeavour* anchored in Matavai Bay where the *Dolphin* had lain two years before.

View of the Baths of Orowhaina in the Bay of Matavai. Otaheite.

A Tahitian drum with carved wooden base, of the type brought back by Cook. They were up to four feet in height, and the drummer beat them while standing

Parkinson's vivid impression of the peaks of Tahiti, as seen from Matavai Bay. On the right is the island's highest mountain, Orohena (7,321 ft)

It was a matter of pride to Cook that except for a few men suffering minor ailments his crew remained as healthy as when they had left England about nine months before. Rightly he attributed this to the fact that on alternate days the diet for all hands had included portable soup and pickled cabbage (sauerkraut) and that whenever a man showed the slightest sign of scurvy he was at once given malt. At first some of the crew had revolted against the sauerkraut, and Cook's method of winning them over was typical. He had it served every day to his officers, who loudly praised its excellence, and within a week his men were scoffing it up so avidly that supplies had to be rationed.

The ship's company were as enchanted by their first close sight of Tahiti's lush palm-fringed shores and soaring mountains as the men of the *Dolphin* had been, and as all but the most world-weary travellers still are today. With an artist's observation Parkinson wrote: 'The land appeared as uneven as a piece of crumpled paper, being divided irregularly into hills and valleys; but a beautiful verdure covered both, even to the tops of the highest peaks.' Even before anchor had been dropped the ship was surrounded by canoes laden for trade with breadfruit, bananas and coconuts. The *Dolphin* men were recognised immediately, and there were excited shouts of 'Taio', which means friend.

Cook, Banks and a large party went ashore almost at once. They were received at first with some caution, but an exchange of plantain fronds soon satisfied the natives that the intentions of the newcomers were peaceable. With Gore as guide they walked four or five miles through deep-shaded groves of coconut and breadfruit trees. Banks was enthralled. It was, he wrote, 'the truest picture of an arcadia the imagination can form', and already in his mind he and his companions were to be its kings. They were anxious to meet Purea, whom the *Dolphin*'s people had believed to be the queen of Tahiti, but there was no sign of her, and the 'palace'

Above Matavai Bay, Tahiti, from One Tree Hill, called by the natives Taharaa, showing the *Endeavour* at anchor and Fort Venus. By Parkinson

Bottom right A Tahitian double canoe with a small fighting platform and armed warriors. By Parkinson

Top right Cook's plan of Tahiti. Matavai Bay and Point Venus are on the far north coast. To their left is the district and harbour of Pare, on which the island's capital, Papeete, now stands. On the north coast of Tiarreboo (Tahiti-iti) is Vaitepiha Bay, off which Cook was nearly wrecked on his second voyage.

in which she had entertained Captain Wallis had disappeared. Molyneux noted that the population of the area had declined and that those who remained were mostly of the poorer class. 'The whole place seems to have undergone a general change in almost every respect,' he wrote.

Warned by the *Dolphin*'s men that trade could easily get out of hand, Cook issued regulations to control it. He forbade indiscriminate barter, and warned his crew that 'no sort of iron or cloth or other useful or necessary articles are to be given for anything but provisions'. But the Tahitians had apparently also made a few rules. Gone were the days when a single large nail would have bought anything from a large hog to a girl's favour. Now for even a small pig at least a hatchet was demanded, and the armourer was kept busy fashioning these from the iron which had been brought along as ballast. To the delight of the seamen, however, the girls showed a great fondness for cut-glass beads which could hardly

be classed as 'necessary articles', and so, without any rules being broken, fraternisation of a kind wryly described by Molyneux as 'by no means platonic' was soon well under way.

As the *Dolphin*'s people had already warned, the Tahitians soon proved themselves brazen and accomplished thieves. On their second day ashore both Solander and Dr Monkhouse had their pockets picked, the one losing a spyglass and the other a snuff-box. Cook took a firm stand, and on his insistence the articles were returned. Next day there was a more serious incident. A native stole a sentry's musket and was shot dead as he ran away. Cook deeply regretted the affair, and Banks, a stranger to sudden violent death, felt an almost personal sense of guilt.

The *Endeavour* drew its water from a stream which ran parallel with and close to the beach, and on the narrow strip of sand between the two a 'fort' was built, with shallow ditches and breastworks topped by palisades on

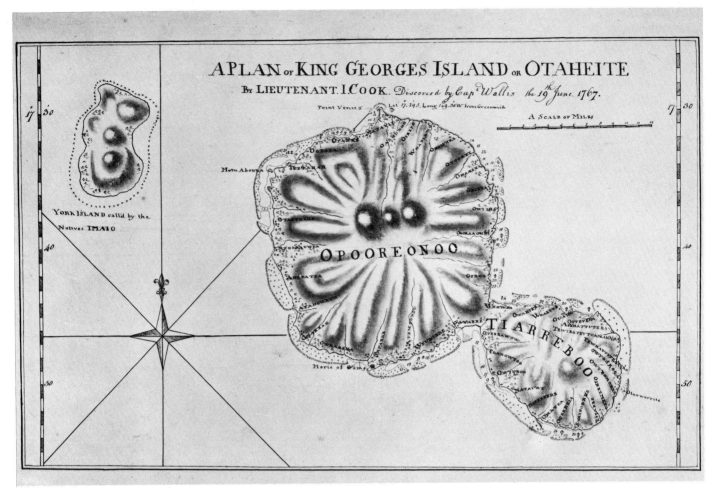

A PLAN OF KING GEORGES ISLAND OR OTAHEITE
BY LIEUTENANT. I. COOK. Discover'd by Cap.t Wallis the 19.th June. 1767.

YORK ISLAND call'd by the Natives IMAIO

OPOOREONOO

TIARREBOO

three sides and a double row of casks to protect the river frontage. Natives helped in the work. They were a little apprehensive when some small guns were brought ashore, but accepted Cook's assurance that these were purely for protection against thieves. Within the enclosure tents and marquees were erected, with a kitchen, an armourer's forge and an observatory.

On 16th April Buchan suffered another epileptic fit. He died next morning and was buried at sea. 'My airy dreams of entertaining my friends in England with the scenes that I am to see here are now vanished,' Banks wrote; but in fact he had little cause for worry, for the extra burden thus placed on Parkinson was borne well, and Banks returned home with no lack of graphic records.

Despite the thieving habits of the Tahitians, all on board found them singularly attractive, likeable and in many ways civilised. Cook was particularly impressed by their fine white teeth, their graceful gait, their scrupulous cleanliness—they bathed three times a day— and their 'open, affable and courteous behaviour' to strangers and to each other. Banks and his party and some of the officers tried hard to learn the language, and Parkinson did so well that he was able to compile a sizeable vocabulary.

Because of the fertility of the island the Tahitians had ample leisure and they had many pastimes such as canoe racing, wrestling, archery and dancing. But the one which most impressed Banks was surfing and surfboard riding. He watched them at it among breakers so huge that he was sure no European boat could have survived. 'Whenever a surf broke near them they dived under it with infinite ease, rising up on the other side,' he wrote. 'But their chief amusement was carried on by the stern of an old canoe. With this before them they swam out as far as the outermost breach. Then one or two would get into it and opposing the blunt end to the breaking wave were hurried in with incredible swiftness, sometimes almost ashore.' This seems to dispose of later claims that surfboard riding was an invention of the Hawaiians.

A mystery was solved on 28th April when Purea made her first appearance accompanied by Tupia, an engaging and intelligent young man, a priest of the *arioi* society, who had been her lover during the *Dolphin*'s visit and was obviously still a favourite. In the intervening time, it was learned, there had been a civil war in which Purea had lost much of her land and power. She was still treated with respect, but certainly had no royal authority. Parkinson described her as 'a fat, bouncing, good-looking dame'. Cook found her 'like most of the other women, very masculine', a rather surprising generalisation with which few of his crew would have agreed.

In preparation for the transit of Venus Cook sent a party led by Hicks to a point on the east coast and

Left A patu, or club, carved from bone and used by the Maoris for ceremonial purposes

Above A New Zealand patu, or war club, carved from wood

Overleaf Maoris challenging Cook's men to fight. 'Come ashore and we will kill you all,' they shouted. By Parkinson

another led by Gore to the neighbouring island of Eimeo (Moorea), both fully briefed and equipped with the necessary instruments. On the day of the transit conditions were ideal, the sky clear and cloudless. At the fort Cook, Green and Solander made independent observations, each using his own telescope, and then compared results. To Cook's disappointment their timings varied considerably.

A couple of days later another mystery arose when Banks saw a native with an adze which was clearly not of British make. It was learned that two European ships had visited the island about six months after the *Dolphin*, and had stayed a fortnight at Hitiaa, on the east coast. When a sheet of coloured flags of various nations was produced the Tahitians identified the visitors as Spanish; and with some bitterness Cook blamed these people for having brought venereal disease to the island. Much later it was learned that the ships had been French, *La Boudeuse* and *L'Etoile*, commanded by Louis-Antoine de Bougainville. The question of who did in fact introduce VD to the island has never been finally settled.

Cook was eager to chart the coastline of Tahiti, and with Banks as a companion he made a circuit of the island in the ship's pinnace. It took five days. Many fertile and thickly populated areas were passed, and it became apparent that far from having a single ruler the island was divided into a number of districts, each with its autonomous chief. During their tour they saw the great *marai*, or sacred place, of Mahaiatea, the largest in all Polynesia, of which a few ruins still remain. It stood on a promontory within a stone-walled area roughly a hundred and twenty yards square. Its base was two hundred and sixty-seven feet by eighty-seven feet, and it rose in receding tiers, each four feet high, to a total height of forty-four feet. There were many sacrificial altars nearby with the skulls and bones of. dogs and hogs, but no signs of human sacrifice were observed.

Early in July, on Cook's orders, the fort was dismantled and other preparations were made for sailing. On the 9th two marines, Clement Webb and Samuel Gibson, deserted and fled into the mountains with their Tahitian sweethearts. The natives would give no more precise information than this, and refused to guide a party to where they were hiding. Reluctantly Cook took the extreme measure of seizing several important people including Purea and held them as hostages aboard the *Endeavour*. It was a stratagem he was to repeat often in the future, and it worked. The deserters were returned and the hostages were released. However, Cook took no pride in his victory. 'Thus we are likely to leave these people in disgust with our behaviour towards them,' he wrote with regret. But he had underestimated the Tahitians, and by the time the ship left two days later all had been forgiven. Purea and several others who had been held came aboard, and there were affectionate

Cook's own version of a drawing by
Parkinson of the watering place in
Tolaga Bay, New Zealand

farewells and many tears. Out of consideration for the Tahitians, who could never bear to see a man flogged, Cook postponed punishment of the deserters until the ship was well at sea. Then they received twenty-four lashes each and were returned to duty.

When the *Endeavour* sailed on 13th July after a stay of three months she took with her Tupia and a boy servant, Tiata. Tupia went at his own insistent request. Cook knew he could be of great value in establishing contact with natives elsewhere, but he lacked authority to take him on official strength, and the problem was solved by Banks adding both Tahitians to his own entourage.

Cook had learned that there were several other large islands within easy sail of Tahiti, including Huahine, Raiatea, Tahaa and Bora Bora, and in the next four weeks he examined these thoroughly. The natives were as friendly and attractive as the Tahitians, parties were ashore almost every day, and there was a brisk trade for

provisions. The temptation to remain longer must have been great, but Cook resisted it, and having named them the Society Group, 'because of their contiguity', he turned the *Endeavour*'s head south on 9th August to look for what he already guessed did not exist, Dalrymple's cherished Great South Land.

By 1st September they had sailed more than fifteen hundred miles and were slightly south of latitude 40. Adverse weather drove them north for awhile, but then it eased and they were able to sail south again, well to the west of their earlier course. Far from finding a continent all they saw, except for the limitless sea itself, were seabirds, seaweed, porpoises, a few seals, a water-spout and a comet. The only untoward incident in this period was the death of a boatswain's mate, who drank a full bottle of rum one night and expired quietly next morning in an alcoholic coma.

In latitude 39 Cook gave up the pointless search and turned west. At two pm on 7th October (by nautical

The naturalist Spöring was also an artist of some skill. This is his impression of Maoris in a war canoe defying those aboard the *Endeavour*

reckoning) a boy named Nicholas Young sighted land from the masthead. Cook named it Young Nick's Head and rightly assumed they had reached the east coast of New Zealand—nearly midway up that of the north island—he learned later.

After two days the *Endeavour* anchored in a deep bay where it was hoped to find wood, water and fresh provisions. The natives were numerous—'a strong raw-boned, well-made active people rather above the common size, of a very dark brown colour with black hair', as Cook described them—and their speech was near enough to Tahitian for Tupia to be able to talk to them. Far from being friendly, however, they were insolent and aggressive, and showed little wish to trade. This was their first contact with white men, and they had yet to learn the chastening power of firearms. There were some minor skirmishes ashore in which two Maoris were killed and several wounded. When a fishing canoe came near the ship's boats Cook ordered those in it to be brought aboard, forcibly if need be, so that Tupia could explain to them the visitors' desire for peace and friendship. Not surprisingly the natives resisted. A volley was fired and four were killed. Cook's conscience about the affair was uneasy, and his excuse that otherwise he and his companions would have been 'knocked on the head' must have sounded thin even to himself. Banks was shocked. He wrote that it was the most disagreeable day his life had yet seen, and added: 'Black be the mark for it'. In their brief time ashore he and Solander collected a meagre forty plants, and they were glad to get away from the place. So was Cook. He named it Poverty Bay, 'because it afforded us no one thing we wanted', and the unhappy name has stuck. On its shore now stands the town of Gisborne.

For some days the ship coasted southward as Cook searched for a safe harbour. All that could be found was a wide, shallow bay open to the weather which Cook named Hawke's Bay after the First Lord of the Admiralty.

Te Kaha, Bay of Plenty. It was here, according to tradition, that the first Polynesian voyagers landed in New Zealand

Many natives came out in their canoes. A few were enticed aboard and treated well, but they remained distrustful and wary. Most, however, were openly defiant. Tongues were poked out jeeringly, weapons were waved, and there were fierce shouts of 'Come ashore and we will kill you all'. When some tried to drag young Tiata aboard their canoe shots were fired, and two or three natives were killed before the boy was recovered. The incident occurred off a headland at the southern end of Hawke's Bay, and Cook called it Cape Kidnappers.

As no good harbours were to be found Cook decided to retrace his steps, and on 17th October the *Endeavour* tacked and stood to the north off Cape Turnagain. Poverty Bay was passed and a little to the north another inlet was found which offered a safe anchorage and abundant water and wood. Cook gave it the native name of Tolaga Bay. The Maoris here were much more friendly and trade was brisk. They had little interest in the usual beads and nails, but were eager to have

Tahitian tapa cloth and, surprisingly, glass bottles. The area was heavily wooded and rich in strange birds and plants. More than twenty different sorts of trees were noted, and Banks and his party had a happy and busy time ashore. Tupia talked at length with a priest and found many similarities between the New Zealand and Tahitian religions. However, he was shocked to learn that it was their custom to eat the flesh of enemies killed in battle. Some men and women were persuaded to sing their war song, and their audience was greatly impressed. 'They distorted their faces most hideously,' Banks wrote, 'rolling their eyes and putting out their tongues, but they kept very good time.' Equally impressive was the rich and intricate carving of their house posts and the prows and sterns of their canoes. Tattooing was universal and much more elaborate than in Tahiti.

The *Endeavour* set off again on 29th October, and next day many villages and cultivated areas were passed. The natives who approached in canoes were armed and

A fortified Maori encampment built
on an arched rock in Mercury Bay.
Drawn by Cook from a sketch by
Parkinson

belligerent. Some grape shot fired ahead of them had no effect, but when a round shot was fired over them they turned hurriedly and paddled away 'without so much as stopping to breathe' until they reached the shore. Cook named the nearby point Cape Runaway.

The coast had now turned west, and the *Endeavour* found herself in a wide, deep bay. Its shores were so fertile, cultivated and thickly populated that Cook called it the Bay of Plenty. The usual canoes came out and there was some trade in mussels, lobsters and eels, but the natives were so arrogant that muskets had to be fired to warn them off. A large double canoe—the first that had been seen and reminiscent of those of Tahiti—approached close enough for its crew to pelt the ship with stones, but the only damage was a few broken windows. By this time Banks was satisfied that the main purpose of the Maoris was to demonstrate their courage by insulting the white men rather than actually to attack them. 'We now begin to know these people and

are much less afraid,' he wrote.

A good anchorage was found on the west side of the bay, and on 9th November Cook and Green went ashore with their instruments to observe another astronomical event, a transit of the planet Mercury. While they were away the ship was surrounded by canoes, and a native who tried to steal a piece of cloth was shot and killed. Cook was angry and said as much in no uncertain terms to Gore, whom he had left in charge. He called the place Mercury Bay.

Further up the coast on 12th November Cook and Banks went ashore and were shown over a fortified village. It was built on a high promontory and surrounded by stout pickets. Three sides were inaccessible or nearly so, and the shoreward side was protected by a double ditch, a bank and two rows of pickets, with raised platforms from which the defenders could throw spears and stones at their attackers. Inside the village were more pickets, and it was well stocked with edible fern roots and dried fish. Cook was sure that in such a strong, well-chosen place 'a small number of resolute men might defend themselves a long time against a vast superior force'.

Once more the *Endeavour*'s course lay northward. On 21st November she anchored in what is now Hauraki Gulf, to the west of which stands the modern city of Auckland. Cook went ashore and found a large river with a flood tide which ran as strongly as that in the Thames below London Bridge. Not surprisingly, he named it the Thames. When natives came on board there was the usual thieving, and one was caught in the act of stealing the half-hour glass out of the binnacle. Instead of being shot he was given a dozen lashes. His companions approved the punishment, and later the unfortunate fellow received another beating from an old man who seemed to be a chief.

Point Rodney, Bream Bay and Bream Head were passed and named, and at the beginning of December the *Endeavour* was at anchor in an island-studded harbour which Cook named the Bay of Islands. Much land around the shore was cultivated, mainly with yams and sweet potatoes, and for the first time the visitors saw flax plants. Doubtless Bay and Sandy Bay were added to the growing chart; then westerly gales drove them out of sight of land for some days. By 19th December they were off North Cape, so called because Cook judged from a strong eastern current that they had reached the northern extremity of the country. Again adverse winds drove them far to sea, and they were still battling their way back on Christmas Day, when, appropriately, Cook sighted a group of small islands which he identified as the Three Kings, discovered and named by Tasman a century and a quarter before. In his journal Cook did not mention any Christmas celebration, but Banks repaired the omission. 'Our goose pie was eaten with great approbation,' he wrote, 'and in the evening all hands were as drunk as our forefathers used to be upon the like occasion.' On 30th December Tasman's Cape Maria van Diemen was rounded, and when the New Year dawned the *Endeavour* had already begun her long run down the west coast, following in reverse the route the Dutchman had taken.

By this time the *Endeavour*'s hull was foul with marine growth and she was beginning to leak at the seams. Cook looked for somewhere to careen her but the generally featureless coast offered nowhere suitable. During several uneventful days Banks and Solander were able to examine their botanical specimens and Parkinson made finished drawings of some of his many sketches of people, places and natural history subjects.

A remarkable mountain rising in solitude from a plain was seen on 11th January 1770 and stayed in sight for some days. It was 'of prodigious height, its top covered with everlasting snow', Cook wrote, and he named it for the Earl of Egmont, a former First Lord of the Admiralty.

Left and above Portraits of New Zealand natives by Parkinson, showing their elaborate facial tattooing and ornamentation

All agreed it was very like the peak of Tenerife which they had seen when passing the Canary Islands, and thought it probably as high. They were well out, for Egmont rises to eight thousand two hundred and sixty feet and the peak of Tenerife exceeds twelve thousand.

The coast now turned south-east and the *Endeavour* crossed what Tasman had decided was a wide bight, but which Cook felt sure was the entrance to a strait. Murderers' Bay was passed, so named because some of Tasman's men had been killed there and nowadays known as Golden Bay. On 15th January, the ship came to the entrance of a broad, deep inlet almost encircled by thickly wooded hills, and next day she anchored in 'a very snug cove' near a stream of water. Wood was plentiful and a single haul of the seine yielded three hundred pounds of fish. Some natives appeared in canoes and threw stones, but Tupia soon got on friendly terms with them. The ship was careened and scraping and caulking began.

After he had made a thorough survey of the harbour Cook called it Queen Charlotte's Sound and took formal possession of it and the adjacent lands 'in the name and for the use of His Majesty'. The queen was toasted in wine and the empty bottle was given to an old man who seemed well pleased. Banks and his people botanized so assiduously that they soon exhausted the area and were reduced to collecting mosses. Banks heard his first bell-birds, and wrote with delight of being wakened at dawn by their songs. 'Their voices were certainly the most melodious wild music I have ever heard,' he wrote, 'almost imitating small bells but with the most tuneable silver sound imagineable.'

To satisfy himself that a strait did in fact exist Cook climbed a high hill and looked across the water. On a clear day he went again, this time with Banks and Solander, and its existence was established beyond doubt. On top of the hill they built a small cairn of stones and left on it some durable objects such as musket balls and beads. The cairn has never been found, nor has the hill been precisely located.

At sea once more on 7th February the *Endeavour* narrowly escaped being driven ashore by a racing tide as she made her way through the strait, to which Cook gave his own name. He now planned to turn south, satisfied that he had sailed almost round a large island. But some on board still argued that it could be part of a continent further south, linked by a narrow isthmus. To put the matter beyond doubt Cook sailed north instead until Cape Turnagain was in sight. He called his officers on deck and asked whether they were now satisfied that he was right, and when they agreed he must be he turned south. What he wanted to prove now was that the land south of Cook Strait was also an island. Natives of Queen Charlotte's Sound had assured him it was and had said it could be sailed around in four days, but he had thought this optimistic and he was right.

Left The New Zealand honeysuckle (*Knightia excelsa*), an excellent example of Parkinson's great skill as a botanical draughtsman

Clianthus puniceus, or Kaka Beak. By Parkinson

For several days as the *Endeavour* coasted south a range of snow-capped mountains was visible at no great distance inland. On 17th February she passed what Cook took to be a large island, inhabited but not particularly fertile, and he named it after Banks. In fact it was a wide promontory, now called Banks Peninsula, and on its northern shore stands the city of Christchurch.

During the same day Gore was sure he had seen land to the south-east. Cook and others were equally certain it was only a bank of clouds on the horizon, but Gore persisted. Determined, as Banks wrote, that 'nobody should say he had left land behind unsought for', Cook set sail in that direction, and turned back for the coast only when Gore admitted himself wrong.

For about a week the coastline remained dull and featureless, with no sign of natives. Cape Sanders was seen and named on 25th February. Here the land looked better, green and well wooded, with several inlets that promised good anchorage. Only his anxiety to press on dissuaded Cook from staying awhile. One of these inlets is now Otago Harbour, and on it stands Dunedin.

Adverse winds drove the *Endeavour* well out to sea for awhile and whales, seals and a few penguins were seen. Contact with the coast was re-established, and on 10th March the ship rounded South Cape, thus finally demolishing a theory to which Banks and others had clung stubbornly that the land they had been coasting was part of the ever-elusive continent. Cook assumed the

Above Much of Queen Charlotte's Sound, which Cook made his main base in the Pacific, has changed little in two centuries

Right Cook's chart of New Zealand, which finally disproved the theory that it was part of a continent. Except for two major errors it is remarkably accurate

cape to be part of the mainland, but in fact it is the southern point of Stewart Island.

The south-west corner was rounded on 14th March, and for almost a fortnight the ship ran north-east along a rugged, spectacular and generally inhospitable coast-line behind which lay high mountains with glaciers and large patches of snow. Banks was eager to go ashore to search for minerals, but Cook rightly considered the risks too great. On 26th March an island came into sight which Cook recognised as lying near the entrance to Queen Charlotte's Sound, and the circumnavigation was complete. Thus Cook established that New Zealand comprised two large main islands narrowly separated by a strait. Except for two major errors—mistaking

Banks Peninsula for an island and Stewart Island for a peninsula the chart which he produced was remarkably accurate.

A few days later a conference of officers was called to decide future plans. Cook would have liked to return to England by way of Cape Horn, keeping well to the south to determine finally whether a continent existed in that general area, but the weather and the season made this almost impossible. So they decided instead to continue west from New Zealand until they reached the still undiscovered east coast of New Holland, and, having surveyed this, to return home by way of the East Indies and the Cape of Good Hope.

Cook, Banks and all on board were deeply impressed

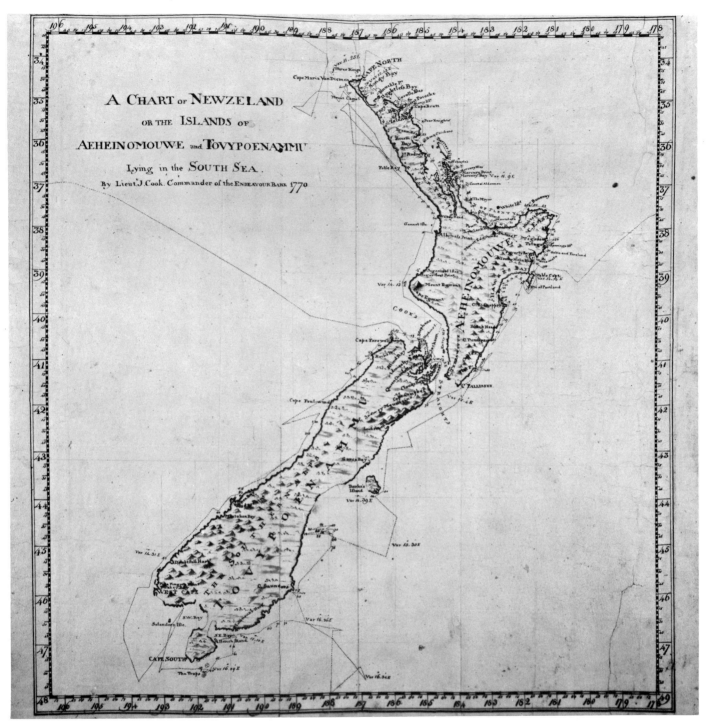

with what they had seen of New Zealand and its people. In language, appearance and many of their customs the Maoris were very much like the Society Islanders and there was no doubt they came from common stock. It was impossible to know whether the New Zealanders had migrated from the Society Islands or *vice versa*, but Cook firmly believed that both groups had come originally from somewhere west of the Pacific rather than from the American continent, and today most who have studied the question still believe the same. Of the two main islands the northern one seemed by far the more rich and fertile, and Cook was sure that European grain, fruits and plants would thrive there. 'In short,' he wrote, 'was this country settled by an industrious people they would very soon be supplied not only with the necessaries but many of the luxuries of life.' If settlements were to be formed he recommended that they should be on the River Thames and in the Bay of Islands, where the land was good and there were excellent harbours. Even though the natives were numerous and often warlike he thought them too divided among themselves to unite in opposing new-comers and he was sure they could be won over by kind and gentle treatment.

It was an age of empire building and colonial expansion, and in view of the enthusiasm of Cook and Banks one can only wonder why such a potentially rich colony continued to be ignored for so long.

Above 'A small high island or rock with a hole pierced quite through it, like the arch of a bridge'—Cook's Journal, 27th November 1769.
In punning mood, Cook called the nearby point Cape Brett, after Rear-Admiral Sir Piercy Brett. It is in the Bay of Islands, New Zealand

Top right Cape Kidnappers, Hawke's Bay, New Zealand, now a gannet rookery. It was off this point that Maoris tried to sieze the Tahitian boy Tiata
Top, far right An obelisk at Kurnell, Botany Bay, marks Cook's first landing on Australian soil

Bottom right A page from Parkinson's sketch-book, showing Australian aborigines, canoes, a bark hut, shields, a spear-thrower (woomera) and a spear. The type of canoe and small paddles identify the area as Botany Bay

The *Endeavour* left New Zealand on 1st April from Cape Farewell. Cook's aim was to reach Van Diemen's Land midway up the east coast about where Tasman had left it. But with this object almost attained a southerly gale forced him to run north and he missed the island entirely. At daybreak on 19th April Lieutenant Hicks sighted the mainland of New Holland near its south-eastern tip at a point which Cook named after him, and which is now thought to be identical with the present Cape Everard. First impressions were good. The land, Cook wrote, 'had a very agreeable and promising aspect . . . of a moderate height diversified with hills, ridges, plains and valleys, and for the most part covered with wood'. Banks judged that it was highly fertile, and every hill, he added, 'seemed to be clothed with trees of no mean size'. Smoke from several fires indicated that it was inhabited but no natives were seen.

Cook was eager to land and as he continued north he looked for a suitable harbour. Cape Howe was passed

and named but Twofold Bay, which would have answered him well, was missed, perhaps in the night. Mount Dromedary, Cape Dromedary and Bateman's Bay went down on his chart. The latter, named after the captain of Cook's old ship, the *Northumberland*, offered anchorage of a sort but it was open to sea winds and Cook passed it by. Then came Point Upright, Pigeon House Hill and Cape St George, the southern headland of what is now Jervis Bay. From the entrance this looked commodious and well protected but the wind was adverse and rather than waste time trying to get in Cook sailed on.

Next day, north of Red Point and in the vicinity of the present town of Bulli, some natives were seen on a beach. Cook, Banks, Solander and Tupia tried to get ashore in the ship's yawl, but as they drew near the natives fled into the bush. In any case a heavy surf made landing impossible, and the attempt was abandoned.

At daybreak on 28th April they found themselves

opposite the entrance to an extensive bay which seemed fairly well sheltered from all winds. This was to become famous later as Botany Bay. As the *Endeavour* made her way in natives were seen on both headlands, but to Banks's surprise others who were spearing fish from primitive bark canoes were so totally occupied that they 'scarce lifted their eyes'. The ship was inside by noon and soon afterwards she dropped anchor under the south shore, not far from a native encampment of six or eight huts. Two boats put off and as they approached the shore two natives came down brandishing spears, shouting and gesticulating angrily for the intruders to go away. Cook ordered the boats to lay on their oars while Tupia tried to talk to them, but their language

was harsh and strange and he understood not a word of it. Presents thrown ashore failed to placate the natives, and they withdrew only when muskets were fired. According to tradition Mrs Cook's young cousin, Isaac Smith, was in the first boat and Cook said, 'Isaac, you shall land first', which he did.

When the party went ashore the same natives approached again, as aggressive as ever. They shouted and threw spears, and it was not until one had been peppered in the legs by small shot that they retired. Cook was anxious to pursue and seize at least one of them but he was dissuaded by Banks, who thought their spear-tips may be poisoned; and the only contact they were able to make was with a few terrified children who

Plate XXVII

S. Parkinson del.

T. Chambers Sc.

Two of the Natives of New Holland, Advancing to Combat.

The Endeavour River, with the ship careened for
repair. This engraving from an original by
Parkinson is the first known landscape of Australia

had been left at the encampment, and to whom they
gave some beads.

The natives obviously had little in common with those
of Tahiti and New Zealand, and seemed to be of an
inferior race altogether. Although blacker than any
others previously seen they were certainly not negroes.
Their beards and hair were thick and bushy, Banks
wrote, and they were lean, active and nimble. None
appeared to be tattooed, but some had painted their
bodies, thighs and legs with broad streaks of white.
He called their spears 'pikes' and mistook the woomeras
(throwing sticks) and boomerangs they carried for
'scimitars'. Cook noted that they wore neither clothes
nor ornaments, and that they lived in small groups

rather than in a community.

Some water was found by digging in the sand near the
anchorage, and later a party sent to the north side of the
bay discovered a small quantity in pools. Next morning
again, on the south side, a small stream was found
sufficient to water the ship. While the waterers were
engaged Cook took the pinnace and sailed right around
the bay, sounding and exploring as he went. He tried
every means to become friendly with the natives but
those he saw fled at his approach. Hicks, in charge of
the watering party, also tried to make friends but the
presents offered were not accepted and, as Cook recorded ruefully, 'all they seemed to want was for us
to be gone'. Next day Cook tried again. He followed a

group of natives, but even though he was alone and unarmed they still kept their distance.

The natives clearly knew nothing of agriculture, and although Banks and Solander found literally hundreds of plants completely new to them and to the European world they came across little in the way of edible fruits or vegetables. On the other hand, the bay abounded with fish, and on the first few hauls alone more than enough was netted to feed the whole ship's company.

On 30th April a seaman named Forby Sutherland died and was buried ashore. Cook named the south headland of the bay in his memory, and today a few miles away there is a thriving town of the same name.

As there was obviously little to fear from the natives

Cook now ventured a short way inland, and the more he saw the more impressed he became. He found the land 'diversified with woods, lawns (i.e. grass land) and marshes', and the soil mostly a light, white sand. Because of the lack of undergrowth he considered that much of the country could be cultivated without having to cut down a single tree. A couple of days later he went with Solander and Monkhouse to what he called the head of the inlet, and here he found much richer land with black soil which he thought capable of producing any kind of grain. 'At present it produces besides timber as fine meadow as ever was seen', he wrote. Many people have since wondered how Cook, the son of a farm-labourer, could have been so wrong about the

Left Tahiti's beautiful and sweet-scented national flower, Tiare (*Gardenia taitensis*). By Parkinson

Centre Australia has a bewildering variety of about 500 eucalypts. This one, *Eucalyptus terminalis*, drawn by Parkinson, grows abundantly on the east coast

Right Ant House (*Myrmecodia beccarii*), an Australian tropical plant. By Parkinson

agricultural potentialities of the area, which in fact hardly exist. It is generally assumed today that what he described as the head of the inlet was actually the present George's River and that he went up this about as far as Tom Ugly's Point, where there is some good soil. Certainly he was not alone in his opinion. Parkinson, for instance, described the country as 'very level and fertile', and Pickersgill said much the same. Banks, however, was not greatly impressed and likened it to English moorland.

Fishing in the bay continued to be successful. One haul included about four cwt of stingrays, one of which alone weighed two hundred and forty pounds, and next day two more were caught which scaled between them nearly six hundred pounds. This decided Cook to call the place Stingray's Harbour, and he named it so in his journal. But Banks and Solander had collected so many unique plants that he changed his mind. He thought about Botanist Harbour and Botanist Bay, and finally settled on the name by which it is still known.

Throughout the *Endeavour*'s stay the English colours were displayed ashore every day, and on Cook's order an inscription was cut into a tree giving the ship's name, the date and other particulars. Enthusiastic references to the bay, which he described as 'capacious, safe and commodious', continued in his journal; and his one great regret was that in spite of constant attempts neither he nor any of the ship's company were able to win the friendship of the natives.

At dawn on 6th May anchor was weighed, and the *Endeavour* put to sea again. At noon, about nine miles north of Botany Bay, she passed the entrance to a harbour which Cook thought might offer 'a safe anchorage.' He called it Port Jackson, after George Jackson, a secretary of the Admiralty, and sailed on. He was never to know the prize he had missed. Beyond its headlands lay what Captain Arthur Phillip, founder of the British colony in Australia eighteen years later, was

Myrmecodia Beccarii Hkf

to describe as 'the finest harbour in the world, in which a thousand sail of the line may ride in the most perfect security', and on whose shores was to rise the city of Sydney.

Broken Bay and Cape Three Points were seen and named for their appearance; then they passed 'a small round rock or island lying close under the land' which is now Nobby's Head at the entrance to the Hunter River. Next came Point and Port Stephens, which Cook thought would be safe and sheltered harbour; then Cape Hawke, the Three Brothers and Smoky Cape, so named because of the smoke seen on it from numerous native fires. Cook was impressed by what he saw from the masthead. The country, he wrote, was 'diversified with an agreeable variety of hills, ridges, valleys and large plains all clothed in wood', and Banks agreed that it had 'a great show of fertility'. They were right, for the land they were passing, on what is now the north coast of New South Wales, comprises one of the richest dairying and intensive farming areas in Australia.

Banks's journal entries at this time were brief. The plants he and his companions had collected at Botany Bay had been kept fresh between layers of wet cloth, and all their time was spent examining and drawing them. Parkinson had now become such an expert that in fourteen days, Banks wrote with admiration, he completed no less than ninety-four botanical sketches.

Point Danger, which marks the border between the present New South Wales and Queensland, was passed and named on 16th May. Next day the *Endeavour* passed what appeared to be a wide, open bay, the pale-coloured waters of which suggested that a river of some size must flow into it. Cook called it Morton Bay, after Lord Morton, president of the Royal Society, but in an edited account of his voyages the word was misspelt Moreton, and so it has remained. The guess about the river was right, and on it today stands Queensland's capital city, Brisbane.

Double Island, Indian Head and Sandy Cape were passed and named. Banks was impressed by the extent and variety of the fish and bird life. There were great flocks of man-of-war birds, boobies and shearwaters; and he also saw water snakes, sharks, dolphins, turtles and a large grampus. The land looked fertile, and many large smokes suggested it was well populated.

In Cook's journal of 23rd May appeared the following curious entry:

> 'Last night some time in the middle watch a very extraordinary affair happened to Mr Orton, my clerk. He having been drinking in the evening some malicious person or persons in the ship took advantage of his being drunk and cut all the clothes from off his back. Not being satisfied with this they some time after went into his cabin and cut off a part of both his ears as he lay asleep.'

A determined effort was made to find the culprit.

Left A wooden painted shield from the area of Cooktown, on the Endeavour River, northern Queensland

Above The first published picture of a kangaroo. It appeared in 1773 in Hawkesworth's account of the voyage of the *Endeavour*

Suspicion fell on James Maria Magra, a midshipman, who had previously quarrelled with Orton and whom Cook considered 'good for nothing', and although he denied the charge he was suspended from duty. Magra, who was born in New York, later changed his name to Matra and joined the British consular service. He was the author of a plan to colonize New South Wales, and the Sydney suburb of Matraville perpetuates his name.

A small harbour with a freshwater stream was found next day and a party went ashore. The presence of mangroves and pandanus palms, the first they had seen, confirmed that they were now passing into the tropic zone, and Banks assumed with regret that from now on most of the botanical specimens he found would probably be already known in Europe. Flocks of pelicans were seen, but kept well out of gunshot range. However, a bustard as large as a good turkey was shot, and Cook named the spot Bustard Bay.

The *Endeavour* continued northward through remarkably calm seas, with innumerable small islands on her starboard side as far as the eye could see. Beyond the horizon, although Cook could not know it, lay the southern end of that immense and fantastic coral wall known today as the Great Barrier Reef, and it was on this that the huge rollers coming in from the open Pacific spent most of their force.

The tropic zone was entered at Cape Capricorn, near the present town of Rockhampton. From then on new names appeared daily in Cook's journal—Cape Manifold, Keppel Bay, Cape Townshend, Thirsty Sound (because no water could be found there), Pier Head, Broad Sound, Cape Palmerston, Bay of Inlets, Cape Hillsborough, Cape Conway and Repulse Bay, the last five all near the present town of Mackay.

On Whitsunday, 4th June, the *Endeavour* entered the passage to which Cook gave that name. He found it 'one continued safe harbour', with good anchorage everywhere. The beautiful islands which form the passage he named the Cumberland Group. With unflagging zeal the names continued to appear—Cape Gloucester, Holburn Isle, Edgecumbe Bay, Cape Upstart, Cleveland Bay, Magnetical Island (because the compass would not traverse well when near it), Point Hillick, Iron Head, Rockingham Bay, Cape Sandwich, Halifax Bay, Dunk Isle, Cape Grafton, Green Island, Trinity Bay (near the modern town of Cairns) and so to Cape Tribulation, so named because, as Cook wrote, 'here began our troubles'. He could have put it more strongly, for over the last six hundred miles he had already been in trouble enough, groping his way through a sea so strewn with islets, rocks, shoals and reefs that only constant vigilance and superb seamanship had saved the ship a dozen times from disaster.

However, it was to come soon enough. At this point the Barrier Reef bends in sharply towards the coast, and at sunset on 11th June Cook got his first sight of a coral

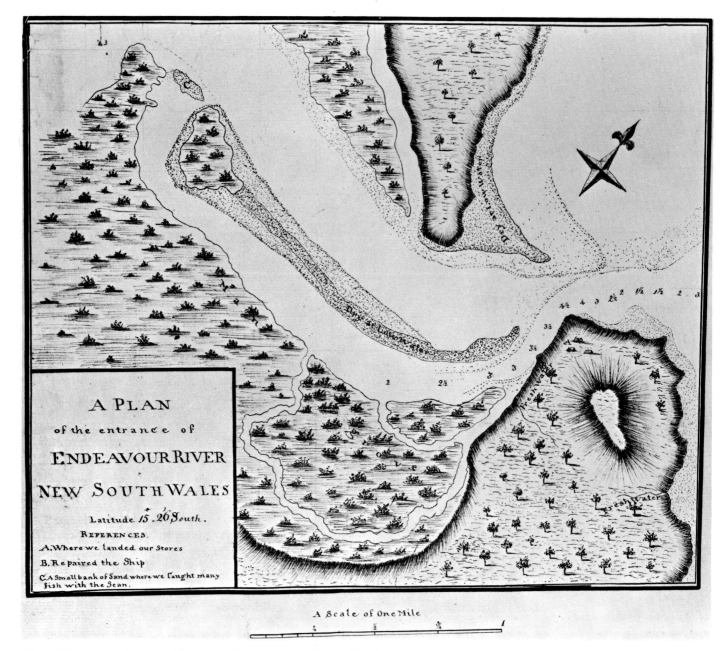

A PLAN

of the entrance of

ENDEAVOUR RIVER

NEW SOUTH WALES

Latitude 15.26 South.

REFERENCES.

A. Where we landed our Stores

B. Repaired the Ship

C. A Small bank of Sand where we caught many
fish with the Sean.

A Scale of One Mile

shoal. He treated it warily and all seemed well until about 11 pm when, without warning, the ship struck with a great jarring jolt and was held fast, pounded by heavy seas from outside the reef. The tide was full and falling, and the only hope of getting off was to wait until it rose again. It was impossible to know what damage had been caused below decks, for water was already pouring in at an alarming rate. The pumps were manned, and guns, ballast, casks, decayed stores and other articles totalling about fifty tons were thrown overboard to lighten ship. Even in this acute crisis Cook was cool enough to order buoys to be attached to the jettisoned guns in the hope of recovering them later.

Dawn came and the morning tide rose, but it was not high enough by about eighteen inches to float the ship. The water was gaining, the men at the pumps were exhausted, and with the mainland about twenty miles away and not enough boats to carry the whole ship's company ashore the position seemed desperate. However,

there was no panic. Officers and men worked calmly to the point of exhaustion, then rested awhile and went back to their jobs. Banks had a special word of praise for the seamen. They worked, he wrote, 'with surprising cheerfulness and alacrity, with no grumbling or growling to be heard—no, not even an oath (though the ship in general was as well furnished with them as most in His Majesty's service)'.

Cook knew the night tide would be higher, so more heavy articles were thrown overboard and anchors were put out to help heave the ship clear at the right moment. At worst this would mean that the ship would founder at once; at best Cook hoped that he may be able to beach her somewhere and build a smaller ship from her timbers that would get them as far as the East Indies. As the tide rose the leak increased. Two more pumps were manned, but only one would work. By nine pm the ship, which had heeled over at low water, had righted herself. Those who could be spared from

the pumps manned the capstan and windlass. Soon after ten pm at full tide the effort was made, and the ship was heaved off the reef and into deep water. To the intense relief of all she showed no sign of foundering. In fact, so long as the pumps were kept going the gain of water in the hold was only slight. What had happened, as they discovered later, was that a large piece of coral had broken off the reef and had stayed in the timbers and partly plugged the hole.

It was now decided to 'fother' the ship, and Cook entrusted the supervision of this to young Jonathan Monkhouse, the only one on board who had actually seen the method used. A quantity of oakum and finely chopped wool were mixed and sewn lightly to a sail. The sail was then hauled under the ship's bottom, and when it came to the leak the suction of the water tore the oakum and wool free and drew it into the leak, where it acted as a sort of plug. The operation was so effective that from then on only one pump was needed to keep the water at bay.

An hour earlier every man in the ship had been resigned to death. Now all talked eagerly of crossing to the coast and finding a habour where the ship could be careened and repaired. By dawn the *Endeavour* was within reach of the mainland. Boats were sent out to look for a suitable place and returned with the heartening news that the mouth of a river had been found not far to the north. Because of adverse winds, however, three days went by before Cook would risk an entry. The channel was narrow and shallow, and when at last the ship nosed her way in she ran aground twice. But each time she floated free with no damage, and by evening she was moored safely within twenty feet of the shore. Cook named the stream the Endeavour River, and on the spot where his ship was beached and repaired now stands Cooktown.

It was a desolate enough place, the soil sandy and barren, the riverbanks lined with mangrove swamps,

Above Parkinson's slight pencil sketch of a kangaroo seen in the Endeavour River area

Above right An unknown artist's impression of one of the *Endeavour*'s company and a New Zealand Maori haggling over the barter-price of a lobster

Below right For a long time it was thought that a picture of a kangaroo in the first published edition of Cook's Voyages was by Sydney Parkinson. It is now established that it was engraved from an oil-painting by the famous artist George Stubbs, for which his model was a skin brought to England by Banks

but the ship's company was in no mood to be critical. She was warped ashore, unloaded, and the carpenters went to work. Banks and Solander botanized, and parties combed the river and nearby countryside for food. Fish were plentiful. Boatloads of mussels were collected, so large that each made a full meal for two men. On nearby reefs turtles up to three hundred pounds each abounded and were easy to catch. There were great flocks of pigeons and crows, crocodiles in the river and vast anthills up to eight feet high. A seaman reported seeing a strange creature which was 'as black as the devil and had two horns on its head', almost certainly a giant fruit-bat or flying fox. Magra saw what he swore was a wolf but was probably a dingo. But most intriguing of all were the numerous reports which came back to the camp of an animal, greyish in colour and large-tailed which moved with the grace and speed of a greyhound, not on all fours but on its hind legs in gigantic leaps. At last Gore managed to shoot a young one of about thirty-

eight pounds which proved to be 'excellent meat'. Banks was fascinated. 'What to liken him to I could not tell,' he wrote. 'Nothing certainly that I have seen at all resembles him'. The natives called these strange creatures kangaroos.

The repairs to the *Endeavour* were soon finished, but it took about a week to refloat her, and for another month persistent south-east winds prevented an exit from the harbour. Cook chafed at the delay, but Banks welcomed it as an opportunity to get to know the local natives. At first they had been as shy as those at Botany Bay, but as they got accustomed to the presence of the white strangers their timidity lessened. Tupia was the first to win their confidence, and in time a few were even persuaded aboard the ship. There was an angry scene when they asked for and were refused a turtle. In retaliation they set fire to some dry grass, hoping to destroy the tents and stores still ashore. Muskets were fired, one was wounded, but good relations were restored.

Cook's attitude towards these people is well expressed in a letter which he wrote later to his old friend John Walker. 'They may appear to some to be the most wretched upon earth, but in reality they are far happier than we Europeans; being wholly unacquainted not only with the superfluous but with the necessary conveniences they are happy in not knowing the use of them,' he declared. 'They live in a tranquility which is not disturbed by the inequality of condition; the earth and sea of their own accord furnish them with all things necessary to life; they covet not magnificent houses, household stuff &c; they sleep as sound in a small hovel or even in the open as the king in his palace on a bed of down'.

On 6th August the *Endeavour* was at sea again. She was still in a bad state, provisions were short, and Cook had the prospect before him of what he called 'the most dangerous navigation that perhaps ship was ever in'. Moreover, to have any chance of reaching Batavia, the main Dutch port in the East Indies, he had to gamble on whether there was or was not a passage between New Holland and New Guinea. He knew that the Spanish navigator Luis Vaez de Torres was supposed to have found one in 1606, but the booklet which revealed this was not to be relied upon, and he could not be positive until he saw for himself.

With the pinnace out ahead sounding and Cook himself at the masthead the *Endeavour* crawled for more

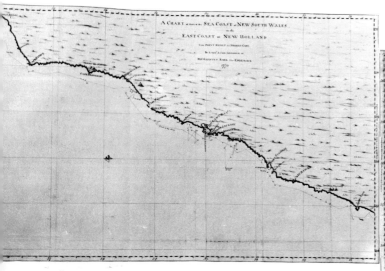

Left Among many rare manuscripts in the British Museum is a book of Cook's charts, plans, views and drawings made during the voyage of the *Endeavour*. This is Cook's own decorative frontispiece

Below and right Sectional charts by Cook of the east coast of Australia. The first is from Point Hicks, where land was first sighted, to Smoky Cape, on the north coast of the present State of New South Wales; the second is from Smoky Cape to Cape Townsend (Queensland); the third is from Cape Townsend to Cape Tribulation, beyond which the *Endeavour* went aground on a coral reef; and the fourth is from Cape Tribulation to the tip of Cape York, showing Possession Island, on which Cook claimed the whole east coast for England

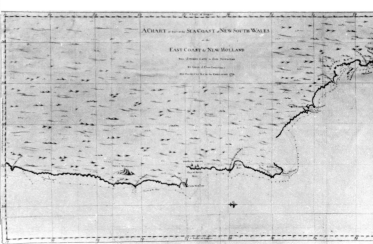

than a week through a maze of hazards, mostly coral reefs, which Cook called The Labyrinth. Then, sick of the whole business, he saw a gap in the coral and went through it into the open sea. It was a great relief to all on board to find themselves in the safety of deep water again. From Cook's viewpoint the big disadvantage was that from such a distance offshore it was impossible to continue charting the coast. Moreover, if Torres's strait did exist there was every chance of overshooting it. So he looked for and found another opening in the reef. It was narrow and the ship approached it as the tide was ebbing. Soon the wind dropped to a flat calm, and some anxious hours followed as the tide turned and began to draw the *Endeavour* slowly but inexorably towards the reef, until only the trough of a single wave separated her from disaster. But the danger passed, another wider opening was found, and the ship went through, driven hard by the flooding tide as though through a mill-race.

Now began again the weary business of threading a way through shoals and reefs. But this time it was not to last for long. On 22nd August it was noticed that the mainland had become so narrow that water could be seen beyond it. Then, a little further ahead, land which

Cook had thought to be part of the main proved instead to be an island, and a supposed bay revealed itself as a channel. Through this a swell coming in from the south-west convinced him rightly that he had reached the far northern tip of the continent. He called the long penin-

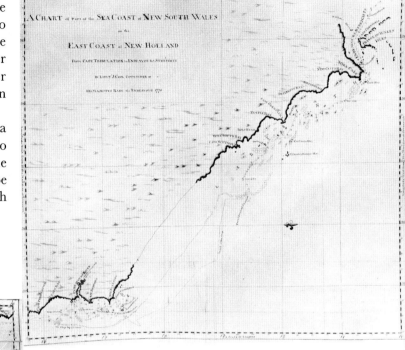

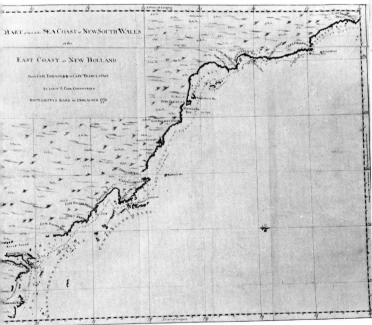

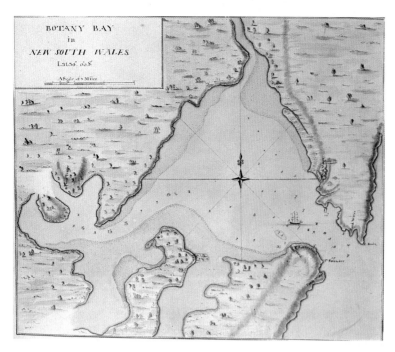

Left Cook's chart of Botany Bay, New South Wales, a typical example of his skilled and careful draughtsmanship

Below Cook's landing at Botany Bay was opposed briefly by two courageous aborigines. This painting of the incident, by E. Phillips Fox, is in the National Gallery of Victoria

Right *Banksia serrata*, or red honeysuckle, one of hundreds of unique plants found by Banks which induced Cook to name the place Botany Bay. Drawing by Parkinson

sula Cape York 'in honour of his late Royal Highness', and warily but with restrained excitement he turned the *Endeavour*'s head west. The coral reefs were behind now, but there were still treacherous shoals ahead and again the pinnace led the way. Cook landed on a small island, hoisted the English colours and took possession of the whole eastern coast in the name of King George III. Three volleys were fired and answered from the ship. Cook called the spot Possession Island and the passage, which lay well to the south of that discovered by Torres, Endeavour Strait. Within another day or so the ship was clear of it, and the way to Batavia lay open.

The rest of the story of the voyage is tragic. Batavia, which was reached on 11th October, was at that time notorious as one of the unhealthiest places on earth. It was low-lying with filthy, stagnant canals in almost every street. According to Banks of every hundred soldiers who arrived from Holland on garrison duty within a year fifty were dead, twenty-five were in hospital and not ten remained in perfect health. Malaria was prevalent, but the chief cause of death was dysentery.

Thanks to Cook's anti-scurvy measures the *Endeavour*'s company arrived fit and well, even though they had now been absent from England more than two years. Ten weeks later, when the ship sailed after having been repaired by the Dutch shipwrights, seven men had already died, forty or more were seriously ill, and the only man still in perfect health was old John Ravenhill,

the sailmaker, who made a habit of getting drunk every day ashore. Those who had died were the two Tahitians, Tupia and Tiata, Dr Monkhouse, John Reynolds (servant to the astronomer Green) and three seamen. 'We came here with as healthy a ship's crew as need go to sea,' Cook wrote bitterly, 'and left in the condition of a hospital ship; yet all the Dutch captains said we had been very lucky and wondered that we had not lost half our people'.

Even worse was to follow. In spite of Cook's attempts to obtain fresh food from outlying islands the health of many on board continued to deteriorate until there were barely enough fit men to tend the sails and care for the sick. On 24th January 1771, four weeks out from Batavia, a corporal of marines died and within the next week there were ten more deaths, including Green himself, Spöring, Parkinson and Ravenhill, who was perhaps unable to immunise himself at sea as he had ashore. Banks, himself almost too ill to move and enduring 'the pains of the damned', was shattered by the loss of Spöring and Parkinson. To Parkinson in particular he and the whole scientific world of Europe owed a deep debt of gratitude. His industry throughout the voyage had been remarkable and far beyond what his employer could have expected. It is known that he made altogether more than thirteen hundred drawings, of which about two-thirds were sketches and the rest finished works, and it is probable that there were more which have been lost.

Cook's journal continued to make sad reading. On 6th February died Jonathan Monkhouse, whose fothering had saved the *Endeavour*, and in the same month there were eleven more deaths, bringing the total since Batavia to twenty-three. Cook believed the worst was over, but more were yet to die before the voyage was over.

Cape Town was reached on 14th March. The sick were taken ashore into hospital, and extra crew were engaged to replace those who had died. In spite of Cook's hopes there were three more deaths before the *Endeavour* sailed a month later; and within an hour of leaving Table Bay Robert Molyneux, master, died. He was, Cook wrote, 'a young man of good parts, but had unfortunately given himself up to extravagency and intemperance, which brought on disorders that put a period to his life'.

As the *Endeavour* sailed off the north-west African coast on 26th May Cook recorded the final tragedy of the voyage. 'About one pm departed this life Lieut. Hicks, and in the evening his body was committed to the sea,' he wrote. 'He died of a consumption which he was not free from when we sailed from England, so that it may be truly said he hath been dying ever since, though he held out tolerably well until we got to Batavia.' He was aged thirty-two.

On 10th July the *Endeavour* came into sight of the English coast, and the person who first saw it was the same Nicholas Young who had caught the first glimpse of New Zealand. Two days later she anchored in the Downs. Cook wrote to the Admiralty to announce her return, and the same day he left the ship to report personally. The voyage had taken two years and almost eleven months.

To his friend, John Walker, Cook wrote with a mixture of modesty and pride: 'I have made no very great discoveries, yet I have explored more of the Great South Sea than all who have gone before me, and little remains now to be done.' In truth, his achievement had been monumental. Apart from charting New Zealand and the whole east coast of New Holland he had solved problems on which men had speculated for centuries, and if he had not actually disproved the existence of a southern continent he had greatly narrowed the area for future search.

It is interesting to note that the name 'New South Wales' did not occur to him until he was on his way home from Batavia. In his log, which he wrote up from day to day, he stated merely that he had taken possession 'of the country' which comprised the east coast of New Holland. In a copy of his journal which he sent on ahead from Batavia he called it 'New Wales'; and it is only in his own holograph journal that this is crossed out and the words 'New South Wales' appear. So it has remained.

The *Resolution* and *Adventure* in the Downs, by Francis Holman. The ships are shown in broadside and stern view. In right background is the *Scorpion*, to which Cook was commissioned briefly before his second voyage; and the yacht in left foreground is that of Sir George Saville, Bart.

THE SECOND VOYAGE 1772-1775

Cook came home to find himself a national hero, and national heroes are allowed little time to rest. Apart from the time-consuming red tape involved in handing over the *Endeavour* his crowded days included numerous meetings at the Admiralty and with members of the Royal Society, an hour-long audience with the king and interminable discussions with Dr John Hawkesworth, a pompous scholar who had wangled for himself a commission to write an official account of the voyage for publication. Banks and Solander were the social lions of London and enjoyed themselves enormously, but Cook declined most of the invitations showered on him and preferred to spend his few spare hours quietly with his family. Exciting as his homecoming must have been it was also tinged with sadness. A few months earlier his daughter Elizabeth had died at the age of four, and a son, Joseph, born a few days after his departure on the voyage, had not survived infancy. On the other hand there were James and Nathaniel, sturdy, intelligent boys now aged eight and seven respectively.

The Royal Society was by no means happy with Cook's report and data on the transit of Venus, and earned a sharp rebuke from Cook when it sought to lay the blame on the dead Green. In fact the various observations taken elsewhere had been equally unsuccessful and for the same reason. Seen through a telescope Venus is surrounded by a nebulous haze so thick that not one of the many observers was able to time precisely when its transit began and ended, and so for practical purposes the whole project had been a failure.

Within six weeks Cook was promoted to commander and given a 'holding' appointment to HMS *Scorpion*. This was merely to keep him on the active list on full pay, for the Admiralty had no intention of wasting his genius on routine service. Dalrymple and his supporters still insisted that a southern continent must exist somewhere, and already plans were going forward for another expedition led by Cook, this time to make a complete circumnavigation in the high Antarctic latitudes. On one point Cook was firm. With vivid memories of the near-loss of the *Endeavour* he insisted that this time there should be two ships. The Admiralty agreed, and early in November two which he had inspected and approved were bought—the *Marquis of Granby*, four hundred and sixty-two tons, and the *Marquis of Rockingham*, three hundred and forty tons. Both were Whitby-built barks of similar type to the *Endeavour*, the former larger by about a hundred tons and the latter slightly smaller. They were commissioned under the names of *Drake* and *Raleigh*, but someone felt this might offend the Spanish, who still claimed the Pacific as their own, so they were rechristened *Resolution* and *Adventure*. The *Resolution* was to carry a hundred and ten men under Cook's command and the *Adventure* eighty under Captain Tobias Furneaux, a Devonshireman who had been Wallis's second lieutenant on the *Dolphin*. Sheathing and refitting of both ships began at once, and it was hoped that the expedition might be ready to leave by the following March. With Christmas approaching Cook obtained three weeks' leave, and he and his wife visited his aged father at Great Ayton.

While there Cook rode over the moors to Whitby to call on the Walkers.

Almost inevitably Banks was invited by Lord Sandwich, now First Lord of the Admiralty, to join the expedition. He accepted eagerly and announced that he would take with him 'as many able artists as the income of my fortune will allow, by whose means the learned world in general might reap as much benefit as possible'. The object was commendable, but in fact the adulation of the London *salons* had so gone to Banks's head that he had lost all sense of proportion. As he saw it Cook was to be merely the man who got the ships from one place to another. Banks was to say where they would go and how long they would stay, and with luck he might even be the first man to reach the South Pole. Again Solander was to be his main companion. Dr James Lind, a young Edinburgh physician, was to go along as astronomer; John Zoffany was to be his principal artist with John Cleveley (who was to sail in the *Adventure*) as his assist-

ant; and draughtsmen, secretaries and servants brought the total of his suite to thirteen. It is said he even thought of taking a certain Mrs Burnett along, but this emerged only later.

When Banks inspected the *Resolution* at Deptford he announced emphatically that she was 'not fit for a gentleman to embark in'. On his demand the great cabin was lengthened and heightened and a new deck was laid over much of the main one to provide space for his party and storage for his equipment. Cook could well have predicted the outcome, but he said nothing. When the ship left dry dock she was so top-heavy that her pilot dared not put her under full sail for fear she would capsize and refused to take her further than The Nore; and in a private letter to Banks Charles Clerke, who was to be her second lieutenant, wrote: 'By God, I'll go to sea in a grog tub if required, but I think her by far the most unsafe ship I ever saw or heard of.' Cook agreed, and with the official backing of Sir Hugh

Left On all three of his voyages Cook used azimuth compasses of a type developed by Dr Gowin Knight. The one pictured here, made by Rust and Eyres after Dr Knight's death in 1772, is similar to those he took on his second and third voyages

Right An improved sextant made by Jesse Ramsden. Cook records that he and several of his officers used Ramsden sextants of this type during the second voyage

Palliser, now Comptroller of the Navy, he ordered her stripped down to her former dimensions. When Banks saw what had been done he 'swore and stamped upon the wharf like a madman', ordered his servants and equipment out of the ship, and wrote a letter of bitter complaint to Lord Sandwich. His lordship's reply was polite but unhelpful. Banks then demanded another, bigger ship and was curtly refused by the Admiralty. His final rebuff came in a memorandum from the Navy Board. 'Mr Banks seems to consider the ships as fitted out solely for his use', this stated, 'the whole undertaking to depend on him and his people, and himself the director and conductor of the whole'. After this Banks had no choice but to withdraw.

Zoffany's place as official artist was taken by William Hodges, aged twenty-eight, a pupil of Richard Wilson and already well reputed himself as a landscape painter. Johann Reinhold Forster, a Prussian of Scottish ancestry, was appointed naturalist and his son George went along as natural history draughtsman. The choice of the Forsters could hardly have been less fortunate. The son was amiable enough but he was strongly under the influence of his father, a former Lutheran minister and a failed schoolmaster, who criticized everything and everyone and was soon loathed by all on board.

At the instance of the Board of Longitude two astronomers accompanied the expedition—William Wales on the *Resolution* and William Bayly on the *Adventure*. Both were able men and the Board spared no expense to equip them with the best modern instruments. To Cook and Wales was entrusted a new chronometer recently completed by Larcum Kendall (K1) to check its efficiency in determining longitude. A chronometer is basically a clock, but made with such precision and of such materials that ideally it will keep perfect time in any extremes of climate and no matter how violently tossed about in rough weather. On his first voyage Cook had calculated longitude by the usual method of 'lunars'

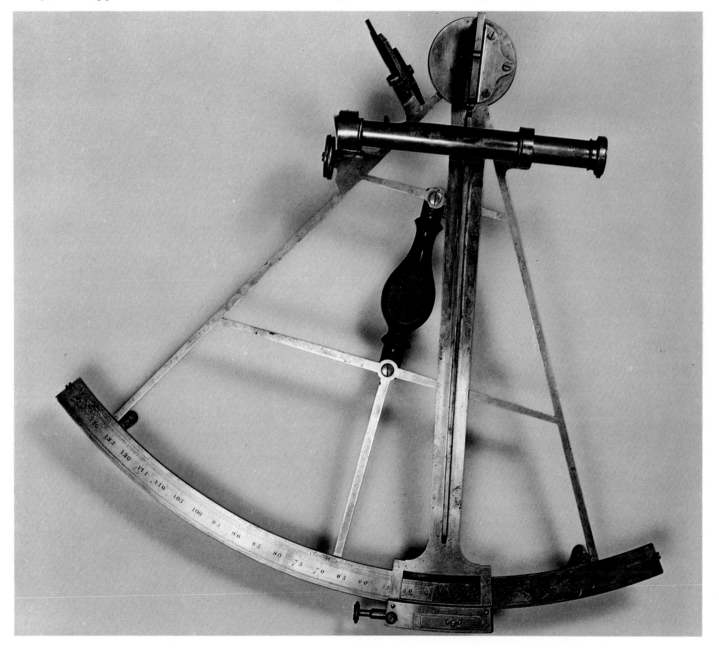

—that is to say by observing the moon at different points in its monthly cycle and then checking these observations against a complicated set of tables worked out for each year. The method was unreliable and could not be used at all when the moon was not visible. On the other hand with an accurate chronometer, set to Greenwich mean time, one had merely to check its reading at noon each day local time, and then calculate the ship's longitude from the difference between the two.

During the protracted unpleasantness with Banks Cook and Furneaux had been recruiting crews for their ships. It says much for Cook that many of the *Endeavour's* survivors volunteered to sail again, and in fact no less than sixteen did. Among them were his second and third lieutenants, Clerke and Richard Pickersgill, who had been master's mate on the first voyage; Isaac Smith, now aged nineteen and himself a master's mate; and two marines, John Edgcumbe, lieutenant, and Samuel Gibson, now a corporal. Gibson was one of the men who

had been flogged for deserting at Tahiti, but obviously he bore no grudge. As his first lieutenant Cook had Robert Cooper, a kinsman of Palliser, 'a sober, steady, good officer'; and as his master Joseph Gilbert, a man of wide surveying experience on the coasts of Newfoundland and Labrador which Cook had known so well. His surgeon was James Patten, and his midshipmen included Henry Roberts, George Vancouver and James Burney. Roberts at the age of fifteen was already a skilled cartographer and a good amateur artist; Vancouver was to earn fame later for his charting of the north-west coast of America; and Burney, son of the famous musician, Dr Charles Burney, and brother of the equally famous Fanny, was to end his career as a rear-admiral.

Furneaux's lieutenants were Joseph Shanke and Arthur Kempe, who was eventually to become an Admiral of the Red. His master was Peter Fannin and his surgeon Thomas Andrews.

Left Marine timekeeper made by Larcum Kendall in 1769, known as K 1, an exact copy of John Harrison's fourth. Cook found it gave the best performance of four timekeepers tested on his second voyage in ascertaining longitude, and referred to it as 'our trusty friend'

Right A letter from Cook to Captain William Hammond, of Hull, from whom the Admiralty had bought the ships later to become famous as the *Resolution* and *Adventure*. It is thought to be the only letter still existing which Cook wrote from the village of Great Ayton, where he spent his childhood

Of the *Resolution*'s crew George Foster was to write later that they were 'savage, brutal, drunken, insensitive and blasphemous'. On the contrary, Cook found them a good lot, 'capable of surmounting every difficulty and danger which came in their way'; and one of his midshipmen, John Elliott, declared emphatically: 'There never was a ship where for so long a period under such circumstances more happiness, order and obedience was enjoyed'.

The refitting of the *Resolution* considerably delayed the departure of the expedition. While carpenters worked on her at Sheerness Cook obtained a week's leave to be with his wife, who was expecting another child. On his return to duty he gave the ship a trial run and pronounced her faultless. The *Adventure* had already sailed for Plymouth and the *Resolution* followed on 27th June 1772 rousingly farewelled to Cook's gratification by Palliser and Lord Sandwich. At Plymouth stores and extra hands were taken aboard. Cook waited long enough to receive word that a son, George, had been born on 8th July, and at dawn on the 13th the two ships set off on their long voyage.

There were brief stops at Funchal in Madeira and Porto Praya in St Jago to take on wine and fresh fruit and vegetables. Aboard the *Resolution* on the long run south through the tropics there was only one mishap when a carpenter's mate fell overboard and was drowned. On the *Adventure* two midshipmen died from a fever contracted at Porto Praya, and Lieut. Shanke was so stricken with gout that he was unfit for duty.

At Cape Town, which was reached on 30th October, Shanke was discharged and sent home. Kempe replaced him as first lieutenant and Burney, aged twenty-two, was transferred to the *Adventure* as second lieutenant. Cook's eagerness to get on with the job was frustrated by the fact that stores which he had ordered in advance were not ready, but the delay was not wasted. The Forsters spent much time ashore botanizing;

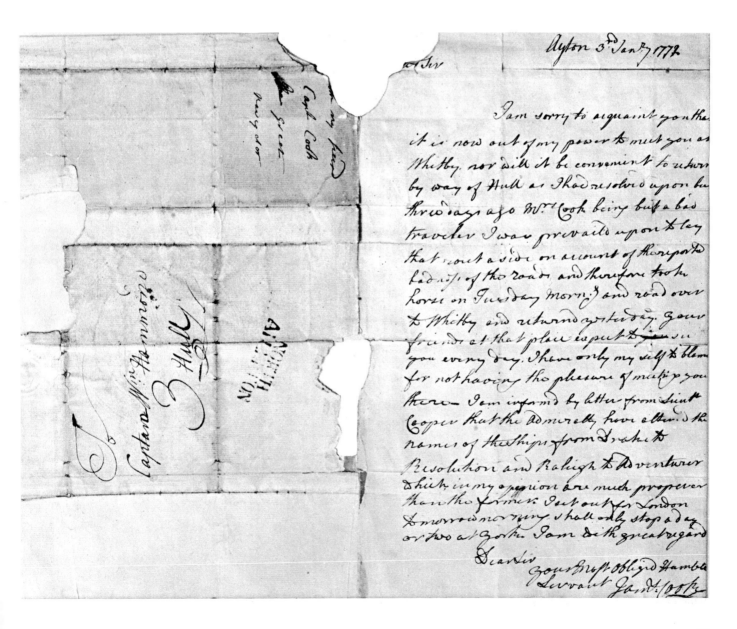

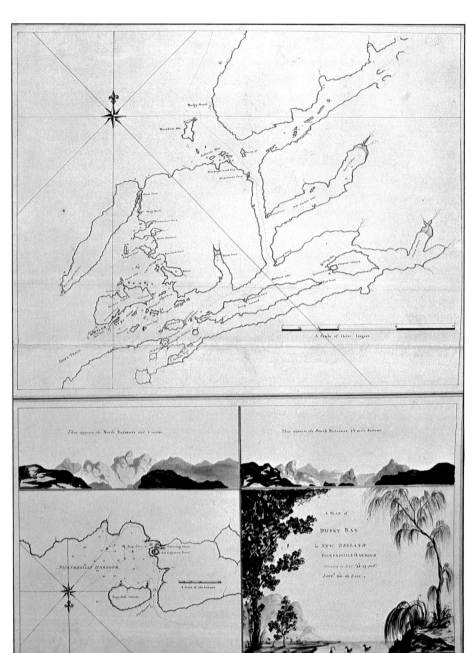

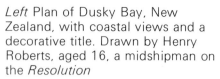

Left Plan of Dusky Bay, New Zealand, with coastal views and a decorative title. Drawn by Henry Roberts, aged 16, a midshipman on the *Resolution*

Below Cook and his companions were fascinated by the huge, mysterious stone idols which they found on Easter Island. While making a sketch for this painting William Hodges had his hat snatched off his head by a native

Left Tobias Furneaux, captain of the *Adventure*. It was painted by James Northcote after Furneaux's return from the second voyage

Bottom left William Hodges, official artist on the second voyage. A pencil sketch by George Dance

Bottom right Charles Clerke, who was with Cook on all three voyages. His letters reveal him as a man of great humour, vitality and courage. Portrait by Nathaniel Dance

Hodges made an oil painting of the town and port which was sent home to the Admiralty; and Wales and Bayly set up an observatory ashore to check and correct Kendall's chronometer and three others made by John Arnold which had been brought along experimentally. The Forsters met a Swedish botanist, Anders Sparrman, a former pupil of Linnaeus, who had been working at the Cape, and persuaded Cook to allow him to join the expedition at their expense. Sheep, goats, pigs and fowls were taken aboard to be distributed among the various South Sea islands. The ships' companies were given a liberal daily diet of fresh meat and vegetables, and when the expedition got under way again on 22nd November Cook was able to report that every man was as fit and well as when they had left England.

Cook's first object was to find Cape Circumcision, about eighteen hundred miles south of the Cape, which a French captain, Bouvet, had seen and named in 1739; and then to locate land which another Frenchman, Kerguelen, had reported in about the same latitude but further east. It was possible, though not probable, that either or both of these could be part of a southern continent. Despite heavy seas and bitterly cold weather Cook searched patiently for some weeks for Cape Circumcision but found no sign of it and decided it did not exist. In fact it does—a bleak, barren and useless speck of land which appears on modern atlases as Bouvet Island. The intense cold wrought havoc among the livestock. 'Not a night passes without some dying,' Cook wrote, 'but they are not wholly lost for we eat them notwithstanding'.

The first icebergs, sighted on 10th December, were for awhile mistaken for land. Every day they became more frequent until the sea was full of them and navigation was a constant hazard. Fortunately it was midsummer, and in these high latitudes there was virtually no night; and the bergs solved at least one problem. When the weather permitted boats were sent out to hack off pieces of ice which were melted down, 'the most expeditious way of watering that I ever met with', Cook wrote. It became increasingly difficult for the ships to keep together, and in case of separation Cook and Furneaux arranged to rendezvous at Queen Charlotte's Sound, New Zealand.

On Christmas Day the weather was kind. Both ships were brought 'under snug sail' in case a gale should spring up while celebrations were under way. Cook supplemented the liquor ration for all hands and 'mirth and good humour reigned throughout'. The Forsters were shocked by the 'savage noise and drunkenness', and Sparrman reported that the men entertained themselves 'by fighting in the English fashion, which is called boxing'. So bemused was he by this 'degrading' custom that he devoted several pages in his journal to it.

By early January 1773 Cook had abandoned all hope of finding Cape Circumcision, and the ships turned

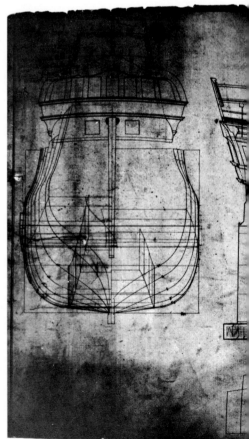

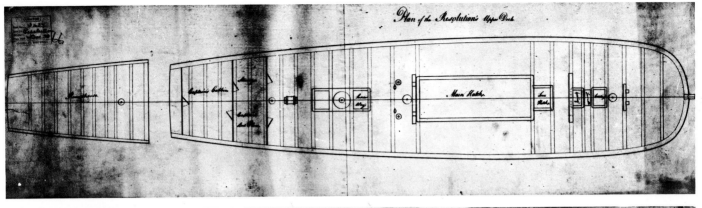

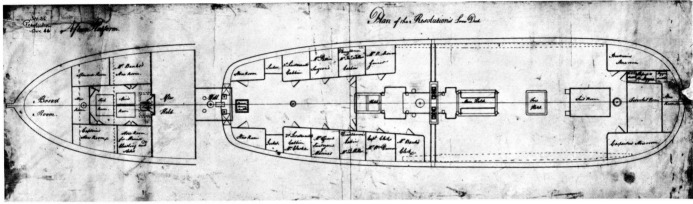

Far left Scale model of the *Resolution*, Cook's ship on his second and third voyages

Above Upper deck plan of the *Resolution* and *centre* lower deck plan of the *Resolution*, showing the additions insisted on by Banks

Below Sheer draught of the *Resolution*. Banks's additions made her so top-heavy that she threatened to capsize during her first trial

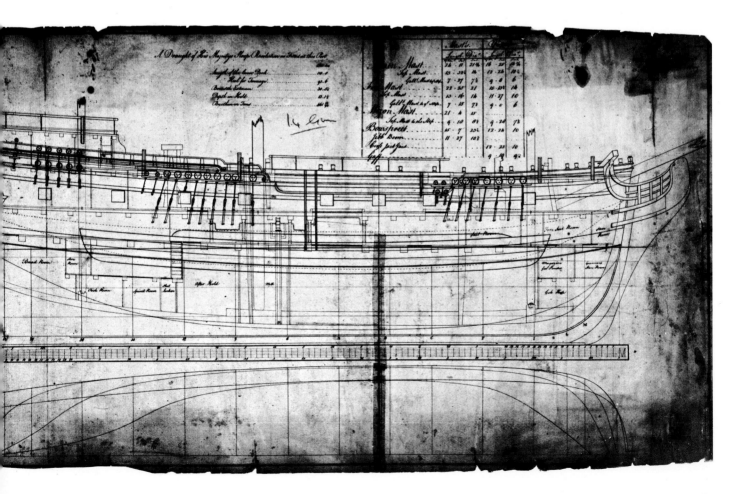

Left HMS *Resolution*, water-colour by midshipman Henry Roberts

Above The *Adventure*, in foreground, and *Resolution* in latitude 61°S,

during their first venture into the Antarctic. The *Adventure* is taking aboard ice to be melted for drinking water. Water-colour by William Hodges

south-east, picking their way cautiously through great masses of bergs. On the 17th Cook wrote: 'At ¼ past 11 o'clock we crossed the Antarctic Circle, and are undoubtedly the first and only ship that ever crossed that line.' Next day they encountered their first pack ice, and within hours it became so thick that further progress became almost impossible. Wisely Cook turned about and headed north. By the beginning of February they were back in the comparative warmth of the forties and had left their last iceberg astern. By now they should be near the land Kerguelen had seen, but a week's search yielded no sign of it.

On 8th February the ships lost contact in a thick fog. For three days they cruised slowly, firing signal guns at hourly intervals during the day and burning fires at night. Then they gave up. Following instructions Furneaux set a course almost due east towards New Zealand. Cook may well have done the same, but typically he steered south-east instead, determined to

probe the polar seas once more. Within days the *Resolution* was again making her way precariously through masses of bergs. On 24th February no less than seventy were counted in a few hours. That evening the ship was in latitude 61°52′, within about three hundred miles of the Antarctic Cirle again and about the same distance from the polar waste that is now called Wilkes Land. To have persisted further would have been to invite disaster, and Cook turned back. But his curiosity continued insatiable, and for another three weeks as the *Resolution* sailed east—through 'dark, perilous, cold days', as Sparrman wrote—he kept her in the general neighbourhood of latitude 60. It was not until 17th March that he finally ordered a course north-east for New Zealand, about a thousand miles distant.

Driven by hard westerlies the *Resolution* made landfall in a mere eight days, and on 26th March she anchored in Dusky Sound, on the south-west coast of the south island, which Cook had passed and named on his first

The *Resolution* and *Adventure*
surrounded by bergs. Water-colour
by Hodges

voyage. She had been a hundred and seventeen days at sea and had sailed three thousand six hundred and sixty leagues without a sight of land; yet only one man was down with scurvy and three others had minor ailments. Cook's official reason for stopping at Dusky Sound instead of going straight on to Queen Charlotte's Sound was that he wanted to ascertain its value as a port and to examine its natural resources. His real reason was undoubtedly to enable the ship's company to rest and relax after their protracted ordeal.

The first anchorage was not satisfactory and the ship was moved to a bay found by Pickersgill and named for him. Here she was able to moor within yards of the shore, and a gangway was made of tree trunks battened together and planked over. It saved a lot of rowing to and fro in the ship's boats. Fish, seals, wildfowl, timber and water were plentiful and easily obtained. Wales set up an observatory ashore; the Forsters and Sparrman botanized in the thick forests; Cook and his officers

thoroughly surveyed and charted the whole sound; and for recreation Cook went hunting, often with Hodges, who made many drawings which on his return to England he developed into oil paintings for the Admiralty. The area was sparsely inhabited, but the few natives who appeared were friendly and harmless enough. Sparrman climbed to a mountain top and looking into the interior saw a vast, fertile area which he was sure would support a large community of European farmers. Despite heavy and frequent rain most of the ship's people enjoyed themselves thoroughly. 'For a set of hungry fellows after a long passage at sea it is as good as any place I've ever met with,' Lieut. Clerke wrote. However, Wales, who suffered from a severe cold most of the time, found it 'a dirty and disagreeable place', and was relieved when the *Resolution* eventually sailed on 11th May.

The voyage towards Queen Charlotte's Sound was uneventful until 17th May when, near Cape Stephens in Cook Strait, the sky suddenly turned dark and

Above The *Resolution* dwarfed by a huge iceberg. Water-colour by Hodges

Overleaf On her way to Queen Charlotte's Sound, New Zealand, the *Resolution* narrowly escaped being swamped by a waterspout. Hodges dramatized the incident in an oil-painting for the Admiralty

turbulent. No less than six waterspouts were counted, and one which came to within fifty yards of the ship would undoubtedly have caused serious damage had it not veered off at the last moment. Next morning the *Resolution* entered the sound and found the *Adventure* at anchor. She had been there more than five weeks, and Furneaux had already had her stripped down in the expectation of staying through the winter. Furneaux reported that on his way he had decided to examine Van Diemen's Land, which Tasman had seen and named in 1642. The *Adventure* had reached there after an extraordinary passage of almost three thousand two hundred miles in twenty-six days. Some days had been spent wooding and watering in a bay which Furneaux named Adventure Bay; then he had coasted north to within about fifty miles of Point Hicks, where Cook had first sighted New Holland in the *Endeavour*. Almost all the way there had been land in sight and from this Furneaux concluded that there was no strait between

New Holland and Van Diemen's Land but merely 'a very deep bay'. His officers agreed, but the astronomer Bayly insisted that much of the land seen must have been islands and that a strong current and swell coming in from the west clearly indicated that there must be a passage. Cook was bound to accept Furneaux's view; but Bayly was right, and twenty years later a ship's surgeon named George Bass was to prove him so by sailing through the strait which now bears his name.

Restless and curious as ever, Cook had no intention of idling away the winter in port. Instead he resolved to explore the Pacific east and north of New Zealand, and to save wasting time he lent Furneaux men from his own ship to help prepare the *Adventure* for sea. Most of the few remaining livestock were put ashore in the hope that they would breed. A ram and a ewe died from eating a poisonous plant, but a boar and sow thrived. Thousands of their descendants are still to be found in New Zealand, known even today as 'Captain Cookers'.

The ships sailed in company on 7th June and for five weeks headed east in the general vicinity of latitude 45. Then, as no land had been seen, they turned north for Tahiti. On 29th July Cook was shocked to learn that one man aboard the *Adventure* had died and another twenty were seriously ill of scurvy, largely because Furneaux, down with gout himself, had failed to enforce Cook's stringent anti-scorbutic measures. Cook had hoped to locate Pitcairn's Island, discovered by Wallis's companion, Carteret, in 1767; but now he abandoned the attempt and made directly for Tahiti. As on the first voyage, several of the 'low and half-drowned' atolls of the Tuamotus were passed, and Tahiti came in sight on 15th August.

This time Cook decided to stop first at Vaitepiha Bay, on the south-east coast, which he and Banks had visited in their circuit of the island four years earlier. The decision was nearly disastrous. At daybreak, with the ships still outside the reef, canoes laden with fruit appeared and many natives came aboard to trade. While this was going on the wind dropped to a flat calm, and despite all efforts the *Resolution* began to drift towards the reef. As a desperate measure Cook tried to get her through a narrow break in the coral but without success, and only a fortuitous breeze from the land at the critical moment enabled her to get clear. Sparrman was impressed by the complete lack of panic among officers and crew, but was shocked by Cook's language

during the crisis.

Although fruit and vegetables were plentiful at Vaitepiha Bay it was found almost impossible to buy hogs. Anxious to obtain fresh meat for the sick Cook lingered only ten days; then both ships moved up the coast to the *Endeavour*'s old anchorage in Matavai Bay. Tents were erected on the site of Fort Venus, and the *Adventure*'s sick were taken ashore. 'Tootee', as the Tahitians called Cook, was given a rousing welcome. Old friendships were renewed and new ones were made. Although trade was brisk hogs were in short supply even here. There were the usual formal exchanges of gifts, the usual excursions into the country, the usual romantic attachments. In his journal Cook denied firmly that all Tahitian women were of loose morals. Certainly, he admitted, there were some; but, he added, 'a stranger who visits England might with equal justice draw the characters of all the women there from those which he might meet on board the ships in one of the naval ports or in the purlieus of Covent Garden or Drury Lane'. Hodges was enchanted by the people and the place and spent busy days with pencil and brush. The Forsters and Sparrman gathered hundreds of plants, but found few species that Banks and Solander had missed.

Cook learned there had been a war with many casualties between the people of the north and south parts of the island, but was unable to discover the cause

of it. He was saddened to learn of the death of an old friend, Tutaha, and surprised that his own news of Tupia's death was received with no visible regret. Purea, he was told, had now lost all authority and was living in such penury that she would not visit him because she had no presents to give. The strong man of the area was now Tu, a Tahitian in his thirties, an impressive man of about six feet three inches for whom Cook soon developed a great respect. In time he was to become King Pomare I, the first of a royal dynasty which was to rule Tahiti for more than half a century. The natives had found their own cure for venereal disease and little of it remained on the island; on the other hand, hundreds had died of another disease—probably a form of gastric influenza—which had been imported about eight months earlier by a visiting Spanish ship, the *Aguila*.

By 1st September nearly all the sick had recovered. Wooding and watering had been completed, the ships' decks were piled with fruit and vegetables, and there seemed no further reason to remain. The shortage of fresh meat still worried Cook, but he was assured that hogs were abundant in other islands of the Society Group, and during the next fortnight large supplies were bought at Huahine, Raiatea and Tahaa.

Cook's object now was to relocate a group of islands to the west which Tasman had discovered in 1643 and named Amsterdam, Rotterdam and Middleburg. If the natives were Polynesian it was obvious that interpreters would be needed, and when the ships sailed on 17th September each had one aboard. Cook's choice was Odiddy (sometimes known as Hitihiti), an intelligent young man from Bora Bora; and on the *Adventure* was Omai, a Raiatean, whom Furneaux proposed to take back to England to fulfil a promise he had made to Banks.

On 24th September they passed two small islands, but did not stop to examine them. Cook named them the Hervey Islands, and they are part of what is now the Cook Group. The first of Tasman's islands, Middleburg (now Eua), was sighted a week later. Hundreds of canoes surrounded the ships as they anchored, and although these were the first white men the natives had seen their friendliness was almost overwhelming. When Cook and Furneaux went ashore they were acclaimed with delight by a huge crowd, not one of whom carried 'so much as a stick'. With other officers they were led to a chief's house, where women sang 'most harmoniously', and natives prepared a drink they called *kava* by chewing roots and spitting the juice into a bowl. It was offered ceremoniously to the visitors, but Cook was the only one who would sample it. Although Eua was smaller than Tahiti and lacked its spectacular grandeur all were enchanted by its beauty. Sparrman wrote of its 'lovely and well-proportioned green hillocks', and Clerke declared that 'nothing in nature could give a more delightful prospect'. Almost every acre was fenced off into neat plots with pathways between. The houses were spotlessly clean, their floors strewn with rush mats. The natives of both sexes wore a cloth wound round their hips and went naked from the waist up. Wales found them 'the most lively, laughing creatures' he had ever seen, but thought that the women, although handsome, were 'rather too fat to be esteemed beauties anywhere but in Holland'. Some considered both men and women handsomer than those of Tahiti, but Cook did not agree.

Their language differed so much from Tahitian that Odiddy and Omai had trouble understanding it. Yet obviously they came of common stock and in many respects they were alike—in the way they made their tapa cloth, for instance, in the restraint of their tattooing; in their grace of movement and sense of fun; in their penchant for light-hearted thieving; in the foods they ate and the way they cooked them. Unlike the Tahitians, however, men and women ate together, and Cook noted with approval that the men were 'so genteel as to help the ladies first'.

Next day the *Resolution* and *Adventure* moved on to Tasman's Amsterdam, which the natives called Tonga-tabu. This was a much larger island, roughly triangular in shape, flatter and not so picturesque as Eua, but equally rich and cultivated. Again the hospitality was overwhelming. There was brisk trading from dawn to dusk, and far from the natives being hard bargainers

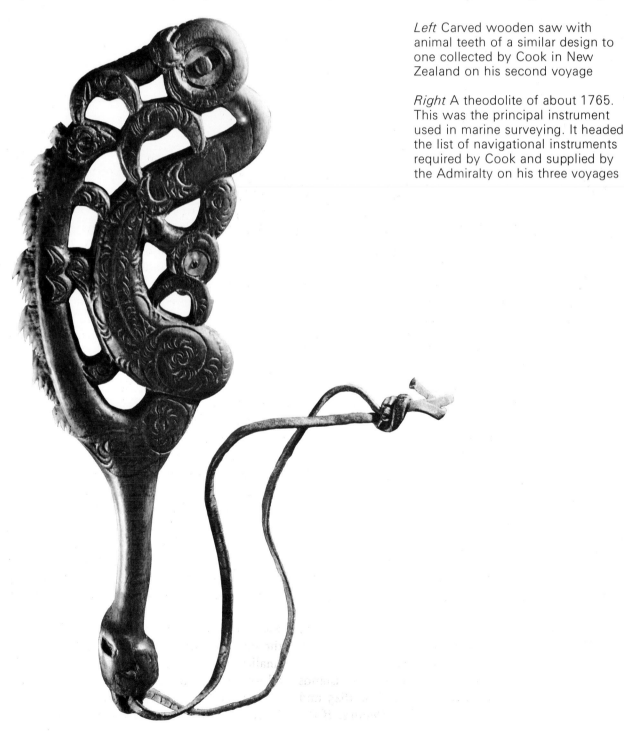

Left Carved wooden saw with animal teeth of a similar design to one collected by Cook in New Zealand on his second voyage

Right A theodolite of about 1765. This was the principal instrument used in marine surveying. It headed the list of navigational instruments required by Cook and supplied by the Admiralty on his three voyages

Cook found them 'more desirous to give than receive'. When the ships finally sailed on 8th October their decks were laden high with coconuts, bananas and yams, and between them they carried a hundred and fifty live pigs and three hundred fowls.

Cook would have liked to examine the many other islands of the group, but with time running out this was a pleasure he was obliged to postpone. Because of the affability of the natives he called them the Friendly Islands, though Sparrman, who saw many war clubs, concluded that the islanders did not always live so amicably together. Cook's name is still sometimes used, but today the islands are better known as the kingdom of Tonga.

The east coast of the north island of New Zealand came in sight on 21st October, and the ships had difficulty in beating down against adverse winds towards Queen Charlotte's Sound, where they planned to refit for their summer probe into the Antarctic. On the night of the 29th, in a screaming gale with mountainous seas, the *Resolution* and her consort finally lost contact. On 2nd November Cook ran for shelter into what seemed a good harbour on the north side of Cook Strait, but lacked time to examine it. The harbour is now Port Nicholson, and on its shores stands Wellington, the capital of New Zealand.

Next day Cook managed to get the *Resolution* into Queen Charlotte's Sound, and she anchored in her usual

spot. There was no sign of the *Adventure*, but Cook was not unduly worried. He waited three weeks, then decided he must go. He left a message in a bottle buried at the foot of a tree, advising Furneaux that after his summer in the Antarctic he would probably visit Easter Island, discovered by Roggeveen in 1722, and then sail on to Tahiti. It was left to Furneaux whether to try to rejoin him or not.

From New Zealand the *Resolution* sailed south-east. The first iceberg was seen on 12th December; three days later the ship was 'quite embayed' among scores of them and avoided collision with one by little more than her own length. 'They say that a miss is as good as a mile, but our situation requires more misses than we can expect,' Cook wrote wryly, and headed north out of the danger area. But it was only a brief respite, and within a few days the *Resolution* was nosing her way south again. On 21st December she crossed the Antarctic Circle in bitterly cold weather, her sails and rigging hung with icicles. Christmas Day came with little chance to celebrate. Upwards of two hundred bergs were seen, some a mile in circumference. 'Had it been foggy nothing could have kept us clear of them,' Cook wrote. According to George Forster at least a dozen men, including his father, were down with severe rheumatics, all hands showed 'a general langour and sickly look', and even Cook was 'pale and lean' and had completely lost his appetite. Again he turned north. A fortnight later, in the comparative warmth of the forties and with the sick list down to two or three, he decided on one final probe. On 26th January 1774 the Antarctic Circle was crossed for the third time, and four days later the *Resolution* reached the incredible latitude of 71°10′, a mere twelve hundred and fifty miles from the south pole. Icebergs were so numerous that Clerke gave up counting them, and ahead as far as the eye could see lay nothing but solid pack ice. Further progress had become impossible. In any case, Cook had had enough. 'I, who had ambition not only to go farther than anyone had done before, but as far as it was possible for man to go, was not sorry at meeting with this interruption,' he confessed; and to the relief of all hands he gave the order to turn north.

The *Resolution* had now covered almost three-quarters of the globe in high southern latitudes in a vain search for Dalrymple's continent. But there yet remained that other quarter, and in the south Pacific there were vast areas still unexplored. Cook had three choices—to go straight home, to winter comfortably at Cape Town for a final summer plunge into the Antarctic, or to see what the Pacific had to offer during the next six months. He had a good ship, a healthy crew and ample stores and provisions, and his own preference was obvious. His officers when consulted were of the same mind; and to his delight his seamen, 'far from wishing the voyage at an end rejoiced in the prospect of its being prolonged for

Left Tu, the paramount chief of Tahiti, during Cook's second voyage. As Pomare I he was to become the island's first king. Crayon portrait by Hodges

Above Odiddy, from the island of Bora Bora, who sailed the Pacific with Cook as interpreter. Crayon portrait by Hodges

another year'. So the die was cast, and instead of easting for Cape Horn the *Resolution* continued north.

Cook's plan was first to search for a large island which Dalrymple claimed, on dubious authority, had been discovered by one Juan Fernandez; then to visit Easter Island; then to refresh at Tahiti; then to locate and examine a group of islands in the west Pacific first discovered by the Spaniard de Quiros in 1606 and partly examined and charted by Bougainville in 1768. Dalrymple's island proved as elusive as his continent, though there is in fact a small island off the coast of Chile called Juan Fernandez. On 23rd February Cook gave up the pointless search and ordered a course for Easter Island. The same day he went to bed, seriously ill of 'a bilious colic'. For days his condition remained critical, and probably only the devoted nursing of surgeon Patten pulled him through. Johann Forster, to his credit, sacrificed a favourite dog so that Cook could have fresh meat and broth, and a few fish were caught to supplement his diet.

He was convalescent and on his feet again when Easter Island was reached on 12th March. It contained no sheltered harbours, but the *Resolution* found a reasonable offshore anchorage. Natives who came out in their canoes were friendly and unarmed, and brought gifts of plantains. Although not prepossessing in appearance they were of Polynesian stock and spoke a dialect which Odiddy could follow. Their own name for their island was Rapanui ('Big Rapa') to distinguish it from Rapaiti ('Little Rapa'), many miles to the west from whence, according to tradition, their forefathers had come. The tradition was obviously sound, for Rapaiti does exist, about seven hundred miles south-south-east of Tahiti, and Cook's midshipman Vancouver was to discover it seventeen years later. Europeans were no strangers to the islanders. From their parents they knew of Roggeveen's visit, which had resulted in much bloodshed, half a century earlier, and a Spanish ship had put in there as recently as 1770. Like most Polynesians they were amiable, they had a sense of fun, and they were great thieves.

Cook insisted on going ashore but stayed only a short while, and next day's party was led by Pickersgill. They found the island barren and treeless, with no animals and only a few domestic fowls and other birds. Potatoes, yams, taro, plantains and sugar-cane were cultivated, but the natives had little to spare, and their only water was too brackish to take aboard. Instead of food the party brought wondrous accounts of hundreds of huge stone idols, some on platforms, some on hillsides, some wearing great cylinder hats, some bare-headed, some standing and some fallen and overgrown by lank grass. They were clearly not Polynesian, and the natives could offer no explanation of them. They had always been there, they told Odiddy, but they had no significance and played no part in their religion. Hodges sketched a number of them, and later incorporated some of his rough drawings into a dramatic oil-painting. Today the stone gods of Easter Island are world-famous, but the mystery of their origin remains.

Soon after the *Resolution* had left the island Cook suffered a relapse of his illness, but he recovered well. A course was now set for the Marquesas Islands, discovered by the Spaniard Mendaña in 1595. On charts they were located vaguely north-east of Tahiti, and Cook wanted to fix their exact position. The group comprises four main islands. Mendaña had called them La Dominica, Santa Christina, Santa Madalena and San Pedro, but today they are known by their native names of Hiva-oa, Tahuata, Fatuhiva and Motane respectively. They are high islands reaching almost to four thousand feet, with fertile valleys separated by steep, razor-backed ridges which come down to the sea, but they lack the rich coastal plains of Tahiti. Their peaks were first seen on 7th April and next day the

Resolution anchored in Vaitahu Bay, Tahuata. Many natives came alongside with breadfruit and plantains, but piles of stones in their canoes suggested their purpose was not entirely peaceful. At first Cook turned a blind eye to the persistent petty thieving of those who came aboard, but when one native made off with an iron stanchion he was fired on and killed. After that the Marquesans were wary but not unduly resentful, and Cook was well received when he went ashore. Wood and water were taken aboard, but though the natives were willing to trade they had little to offer. Once the precise position of the group had been fixed there was no reason to remain, and on 12th April the *Resolution* was on her way again. The briefness of the visit was generally regretted, for not only were the islands spectacular and beautiful, but their people were by far the most attractive yet seen. They were slim, lithe and graceful, of a light honey colour, the women and children as fair as many Europeans. Clerke called them

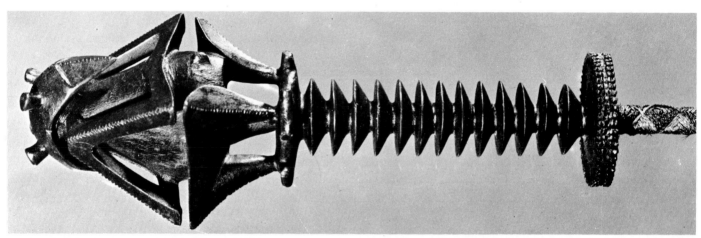

'the most beautiful race of people I ever beheld'. Wales wrote virtually the same thing; and even Cook, staunchly pro-Tahitian as he was, had to admit that 'for a fine shape and regular features they perhaps surpass all other nations'.

Some of the atolls of the Tuamotus were passed on the way to Tahiti, and a brief landing was made on one, Takaroa; but the natives, although not actively hostile, waved clubs and spears to let it be known the visitors were not welcome, and Cook wisely took the hint.

The *Resolution* anchored in Matavai Bay on 22nd April, and Cook and his men were welcomed with joy by many old friends. This time no tents were erected for the sick because there were none. Prosperity and happiness seemed to have returned to the island; hogs, fruit and vegetables were once again plentiful; and Tu, who was still the paramount chief, was much more friendly and accessible than before. Although nails and hatchets were still acceptable what the Tahitians most

coveted this time were the red parrot feathers which members of the crew had brought as curiosities from the Friendly Islands. Cook was not aware that red was sacred to the Tahitian god Oro and that red feathers played an important part in his cult. Nevertheless, he welcomed this new form of currency the more because stocks of the usual trade goods were now running low.

One day Cook and a party which included Hodges and the Forsters went to call on Tu at Pare (the district of Papeete) and were astounded to find the harbour crammed with a vast fleet of double canoes. Cook counted a hundred and sixty huge war canoes with fighting platforms and a hundred and seventy smaller ones which he took to be transports and victuallers. Each fighting canoe was decorated with flags and streamers and manned by about forty rowers and warriors. The warriors were armed with clubs, spears and stones, and some wore helmets so huge and cumbersome that they seemed to Cook 'more designed for show

Top left Carved wooden handle of a Tahitian fly flap (or whisk), possibly given to Cook as a present and taken to England by him

Bottom left A coastal view in Tahiti by William Hodges. Away from Papeete many parts of the island look very much today as they did in Cook's time

Below Omai, who sailed from Tahiti in the *Adventure* and spent some time in England. Portrait by Sir Joshua Reynolds

Right Omai in Tahitian dress. With Banks as his sponsor he became a great success in London society. Pencil drawing attributed to Nathaniel Dance

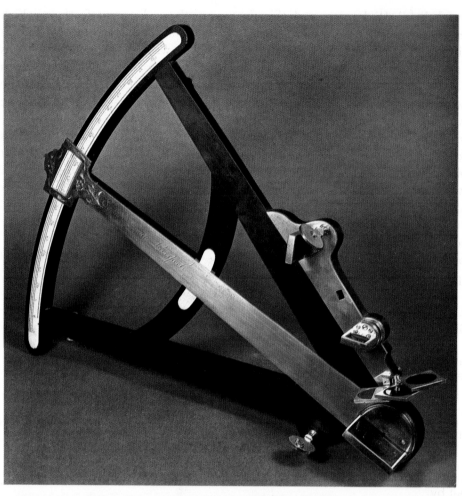

Left An octant made by Egerton Smith, of Liverpool. It is likely that Cook took one similar to this on his second and third voyages

Below A set of drawing instruments and their case, of the type used by Cook and other cartographers in the late 18th century

Top right This painting by William Hodges of the *Resolution* and *Adventure* at anchor in Matavai Bay, Tahiti, gives a vivid impression of the natural beauty of the island

Right below Several natives were killed and two of Cook's men were wounded during an attempted landing on Erromanga, in the New Hebrides. Painting by William Hodges

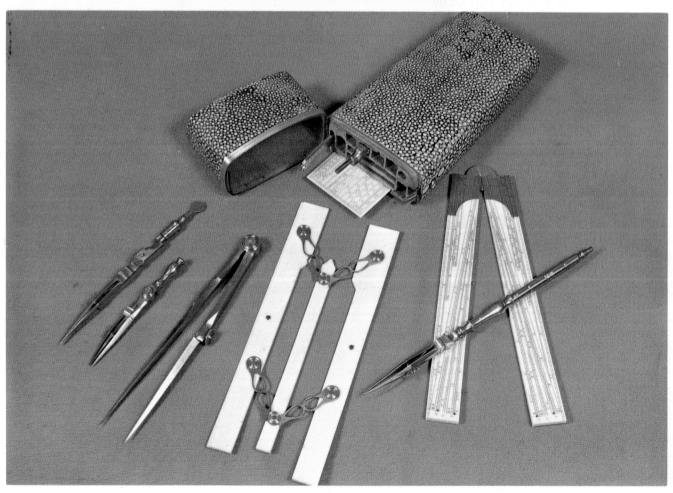

than for use'. He estimated the full complement at seven thousand seven hundred and sixty, and as he was assured that all came from the one district of Atahuru he and his companions had to revise their ideas of the total population of the island. Cook thought it might even run to two hundred and forty thousand; the Forsters were inclined to halve that figure. All were tremendously impressed by the sight, and Cook doubted whether such 'a grand and noble appearance' had ever been seen in the Pacific before. From Towha, the admiral of the fleet, 'a brave, sensible and intelligent chief', it was learned that this was a full-dress rehearsal for an invasion of the nearby island of Moorea, whose chief was in revolt against Tu.

During his stay in Tahiti Wales was able to check that the Kendall chronometer had lost only eight and a half minutes in the five months since leaving New Zealand, a remarkable performance in view of the extremes of heat and cold it had been through.

From Tahiti the *Resolution* sailed on 15th May for Huahine and Raiatea. Trading on both islands was brisk and successful, many old friendships were renewed, and special entertainments of music, dancing and plays were put on for the visitors' benefit. When Odiddy said goodbye to Cook he wept bitterly and begged him to return. At his request Cook gave him a letter which praised his good behaviour and recommended him to other Europeans who might visit the islands.

Left On her second plunge into the Antarctic the *Resolution* ran into thick pack-ice. Water-colour by Hodges

Bottom left One of several drawings by Hodges of Tahitian war canoes lined up for review

Right On his return to England Hodges developed several sketches into oil-paintings for the Admiralty. This one, of Tahitian war canoes, hangs in the Old Admiralty

Bottom right Savage Island, so named by Cook because his attempt to land there was angrily opposed by the natives. Pen and wash drawing by Hodges

Overleaf War canoes of Tahiti drawn up for review in rehearsal for an attack on the nearby island of Eimeo (Moorea). Painting by William Hodges

On 17th June, a fortnight out from Raiatea on her way west, the *Resolution* passed an isolated atoll which Cook named for Lord Palmerston. Five days later a much larger high island of about thirty-three miles in circuit was seen. A party which sought to go ashore was repulsed by angry natives who threw stones and spears, and Cook named it Savage Island. Today it has reverted to its native name of Niue.

The easternmost islands of the Friendly Group were sighted on 25th June, and two days later the ship anchored off Tasman's Rotterdam, the present island of Nomuka. The natives, who knew of the earlier visit, were friendly enough but not so effusively so as those of Eua and Tongatabu. There was some unpleasantness when a native who stole surgeon Patten's musket was wounded, but Patten returned good for evil by dressing the wounds. A day was spent examining other islands in the group, including the active volcano of Tofua, and on 30th June the *Resolution* was on her way again.

Cook's eagerness to explore the islands first located by Quiros was understandable. The Spaniard had convinced himself that the land which he named grandiosely Austrialia Del Espiritu Santo was part of a great continent, and he had dreamed of establishing an ideal Christian colony there, to be known as New Jerusalem. A little later, and independently, his pilot Torres had disproved the theory by sailing round the island. In 1768 Bougainville had examined and charted Espiritu

Santo and several neighbouring islands, which he had collectively named the Great Cyclades. Although aware that many other islands forming a considerable archipelago lay to the south he had sailed on without examining them; and this seemed reason enough for Cook to complete the task. He could hardly have guessed what he was letting himself in for, for apart from the twelve main islands of the group there are about seventy smaller ones, the whole stretching over about four hundred and fifty miles.

Bougainville's Aurora Island (Maewo), the north-easternmost of the group, was sighted on 17th July and in the next few days the *Resolution* cruised among a maze of islands large and small. On the larger ones wood and water were plentiful, and the land appeared fertile and thickly populated. Many natives, armed with spears and bows and arrows were seen, but few ventured out in their canoes. The *Resolution* made her first anchorage on 22nd July in a sheltered bay in Mallicolo (Malekula). Some armed natives came out in canoes and a few ventured aboard. Their manner was arrogant and one aimed an arrow at Cook, who got in first and peppered him with small shot. A shower of arrows followed; then a four-pounder fired overhead sent the whole crowd scurrying ashore in confusion. Cook landed next morning in the face of about five hundred armed men, but there was no trouble. Instead their chief put aside his weapons and offered a green branch as a sign of peace. Little interest was shown in the presents Cook offered, and the party stayed only long enough to gather some wood. The following day Cook went ashore again and he and the Forsters were grudgingly allowed to walk a little way inland, but it was made clear that they were unwelcome and Cook did not press his luck. He found them a singularly unattractive people, flat-nosed and thick-lipped with 'monkey faces', the women as 'disagreeable as the men'.

After ten days of slow cruising, never out of sight of land, Cook decided to chance another landing, this time on Erromanga. He was welcomed by a vast crowd who, although armed, seemed friendly enough at first and courteously accepted the green branch he offered. However, their temper soon changed. Oars were seized and attempts made to drag the boat ashore. Arrows were fired and spears thrown, and it took a volley of musket-fire to drive the natives back. Several were killed, and two of the boat's crew were slightly wounded. Cook did not blame the islanders for their hostility. 'It is impossible for them to know our real design,' he wrote. 'We enter their ports and attempt to land in a peaceable manner. If this succeeds all is well, if not we land nevertheless and maintain our footing by the superiority of our firearms. In what other light can they first look upon us but as invaders of their country?'

Even so, the need for wood, water and fresh provisions tempted him to try yet again. This time he chose Tanna,

Above A stone statue of Easter Island, called Hoa-haka-nana-ia ('Breaking waves'). It was found at Orongo, a part of the island not visited by Cook's party

Top right Marquesan club-head, similar to one taken back to England by Cook

Far right Head of a carved wooden fighting club from the Marquesas Islands

Right Three bamboo nose flutes from Tahiti, taken home by Cook or one of his ship's company. These flutes are still played in Tahiti

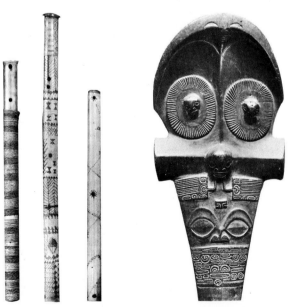

one of the southernmost of the group, a high island of rare beauty crowned by an active volcano. At first the landing was clearly resented but there was no active hostility, and eventually the natives became so friendly that what was meant to have been a brief visit extended to a fortnight. Trade in pigs and coconuts was brisk, some friendships were made, there were daily excursions inland, and good relations were marred only once when a sentry shot a native dead with little apparent provocation. The people of Tanna were of mixed Melanesian and Polynesian stock and were bilingual. They impressed Cook as active and nimble, with 'good features and agreeable countenances'. The men excelled in the use of arms but were not fond of work, and he noted disapprovingly that they left most of the hard labour to their womenfolk.

From Tanna the *Resolution* retraced her course north. Among the islands passed was one which Cook named for Lord Sandwich. It is known again today by its native name of Efate, and on it stands Vila, the administrative centre of the group. Several days were spent examining Quiros's Espiritu Santo; and on 31st August as he left the archipelago Cook wrote: 'As we have not only ascertained the extent and situation of these islands but added several new ones and explored the whole I think we have obtained a right to name them, and shall for the future distinguish them under the name of the New Hebrides.'

Four days out, following a south-westerly course, the *Resolution* came in sight of land again—high, mountainous and apparently extensive. A maze of coral reefs discouraged progress north, so Cook turned south instead. Next day the ship was able to get inside the reef and anchored about a mile offshore. Many natives came out, some in canoes, some swimming, and very few armed. Once their initial shyness was overcome they crowded aboard until, as Cook wrote, 'the ship was full of them'. They were a friendly, laughing people, slightly negroid in appearance but well-featured and attractive. Unlike the Polynesians they were not given to stealing. During several days Cook spent much of his time ashore. With a native guide he climbed to the top of a steep ridge from whence he could see the other side of the island, which he estimated to be about thirty-five miles wide. The central mountain range was barren and mostly solid rock, but there were fertile, well-watered valleys in which sugar-cane, plantains, yams, taro and other root vegetables were cultivated. In several respects, Cook wrote, the country bore 'a great affinity to some parts of New Holland', with its white-barked trees (eucalypts), lack of undergrowth and sandy, mangrove-lined shores. The Forsters found a few new birds and many new plants, including a passion-flower which was thought to grow wild only in South America.

For more than a fortnight the *Resolution* sailed slowly south, establishing that the eastern coastline of the island was at least two hundred and fifty miles long. Cook would have liked to explore the west coast as well, but adverse winds, dangerous reefs and lack of time ruled this out, and early in October the ship headed south into the open sea. The natives apparently had no single name for the island, so Cook called it New Caledonia and surmised that next to New Zealand it was perhaps the largest island in the south Pacific.

At dawn on 10th October a smallish solitary island was seen ahead. The *Resolution* anchored and Cook and a party went ashore. They found it uninhabited and remarkably fertile. Large areas were thick with the New Zealand flax plant, and spruce pines—tall, straight, strong and ideal for masts—were 'in vast abundance'.

There were groves of cabbage palms, ample fresh water, and a great variety of land and sea birds. Cook named it Norfolk Island, 'after the noble family of Howard', and would willingly have lingered. But again time was the problem, and at dusk the *Resolution* sailed on.

Queen Charlotte's Sound was reached on 19th October. The message Cook had left for Furneaux had gone and there was no other in its place; but there were obvious signs that a ship had been there and Cook rightly supposed it to have been the *Adventure*. The refitting of the *Resolution* for her final plunge into the Antarctic began at once. A few old friends appeared, but there was a general air of wariness and reserve among the Maoris that puzzled Cook and his officers.

A rumour that a European ship had sunk in the strait and that its survivors had been killed and eaten was firmly denied; nevertheless, when the *Resolution* sailed on 11th November Cook still had an uneasy feeling that something had occurred during the *Adventure*'s stay which the natives were unwilling to discuss.

Heading east in the general area of latitude 55 and driven by strong westerlies, the *Resolution* covered four thousand five hundred miles during five weeks, her best single day's run being a hundred and eighty-four miles. No land was seen until 17th December when Cape Deseado, near the southern tip of South America, came into sight. She coasted cautiously south for three days, then anchored in a deep, sheltered harbour to take on wood and water and to enable the Forsters to botanize. Because of the season Cook called the harbour Christmas Sound. Geese and other wildfowl were plentiful and every day parties returned with large bags. On Christmas morning a few natives came aboard—'a little, ugly, half-starved, beardless race', as Cook described them—who stank intolerably of rancid oil. They were not invited to stay for Christmas dinner, which featured roast and boiled goose and goose pie with some Madeira wine, almost the only liquor that was left.

View from Point Venus, Tahiti, looking eastward. The small island in the background is Motu Au. Painting by William Hodges

Far left Bearded penguin (*Pygoscelis antarctica*) on an ice floe. Water-colour by George Forster

Left Part of a bird-headed fighting club from New Caledonia

Top right Cook landing at Tanna, New Hebrides. Here the natives, who were part-Polynesian, were much more friendly than those of other islands in the group. Oil-painting by Hodges

Centre right Head of a spear from Malekula, New Hebrides, with separate barb of bone lashed to the head. The more elaborately made and decorated spears were reserved for war or ceremonial purposes

Below View of South Georgia. Cook found this island, east of Cape Horn, to be ice- and snow-bound, bleak and barren. A water-colour by Hodges

The *Resolution* stood out to sea on 28th December, and next morning Cape Horn was rounded in calm and pleasant weather. There was a short stay at Success Bay, which Cook had visited in the *Endeavour*. It was thought the *Adventure* may have called there on her way home and Pickersgill was sent ashore, but he found no sign of her. Some days were spent examining and charting the east coast of Staten Island, and early in January the *Resolution* left the area.

Cook's object now was to complete his circumnavigation in high southern latitudes, and in doing so to look for an extensive area of land which Dalrymple, on his usual dubious authority, claimed had been discovered in 1674 by one Antoine de la Roche. There was, of course, no sign of it. Nevertheless, a few days after he had given up the futile search Cook did find land, much further to the east. It was ice- and snow-bound, bleak and barren, and the *Resolution* nosed her way warily along its forbidding coast. Cook and a party managed to get ashore and found the interior 'not less savage and horrible' than its shores, an area of wild rocks and mountains, their lofty summits lost in the clouds. There was a vast seal and sea-bird population, but not a tree or even a shrub was to be seen, and the botanists found only three plants. If this was to prove the southern continent for which he had searched so long it was 'not worth the discovery', Cook wrote. All the same, he took formal possession of it with an appropriate volley of

musketry, and called it South Georgia. A few days later the *Resolution* rounded its south-east corner to establish that it was merely another island, and Cook left it without regret.

On 29th January, just below latitude 60, other islands were discovered, a string of them running south to north, small, desolate and useless for most practical purposes. Having named them the South Sandwich Group, Cook wrote firmly that he was 'now tired of these high latitudes where nothing is to be found but ice and thick fogs', and resolved to go no further south. Instead, the *Resolution* pressed on eastward for another three weeks in a final vain search for Bouvet's Cape Circumcision, until she had crossed the track of her first entry into the polar regions more than two years ago. The Dalrymple myth had been finally exploded; there was certainly no southern continent except perhaps under thick ice at the South Pole itself. Cook considered that 'the intention of the voyage had in every respect been fully answered', and thankfully turned north.

The *Resolution* anchored in Table Bay on 21st March. Cook went ashore to learn that the *Adventure* had preceded him by almost exactly a year and to find awaiting him a letter from Furneaux. This confirmed what he had already feared. He and Furneaux had missed each other at Queen Charlotte's Sound by only a few days. On the eve of the *Adventure*'s departure

Furneaux had sent John Rowe, master's mate, who was a relative by marriage, with nine others in the ship's cutter to gather wild greens. They had not returned, and next day it was discovered they had been slaughtered and eaten by the Maoris. Sickened by this experience Furneaux had decided to sail for England, and had done so by way of Cape Horn in approximately the same latitudes as the *Resolution*, thus doubly confirming Cook's own findings.

A damaged rudder and other repairs kept Cook at the Cape for five weeks. The *Resolution*'s homeward route was *via* St Helena, Ascension Island and the Azores, and she dropped anchor at Spithead on 30th July 1775. Her voyage had taken three years and eighteen days; and in that time, Cook wrote proudly, he had lost four men, only one by sickness.

The death of Cook, an aquatint by the well-known marine painter John Cleveley, developed from a sketch by his brother James, who was a carpenter aboard the *Resolution*

THE THIRD
VOYAGE
1776-1780

Cook's achievements of the second voyage were already well-known in London from Furneaux's personal accounts and from the journals which Cook had sent in advance from Cape Town. He was now forty-six, he had served his country nobly, and it was generally agreed he had earned honourable and comfortable retirement. The Royal Society elected him a Fellow and awarded him the Copley Gold Medal for a paper he submitted on methods of combating scurvy at sea. Sandwich and Palliser treated him as an old and close personal friend. Banks, all unpleasantness forgotten, made much of him and persuaded him to sit to Nathaniel Dance for what was to become his best-known portrait.

On 9th August he was presented again to King George III, and the same day he was promoted post captain in command of HMS *Kent*, seventy-four guns. It was a purely nominal command for a day later he was appointed a captain at Greenwich Hospital. Although this was a well-paid sinecure Cook was hesitant, and agreed to apply only on condition that he be allowed to quit at any time should he be required for more active service. The appointment carried accommodation at the hospital, but Cook preferred to live at home with his wife and family. The son born soon before his departure had died in infancy; but James, now aged twelve, was already at the Royal Woolwich Academy training to be a naval officer, and Nathaniel, a year younger, had the same ambition.

The Tahitian Omai, who had returned with Furneaux, had been a great success in England. He had been presented to the King, he had been entertained by the nobility and gentry, and during a tour of England with Banks he had met Cook's aged father at Great Ayton. It was now time for him to be taken home, and the Admiralty ordered the *Resolution* refitted for that purpose. Cook's reaction was predictable. On 19th August he wrote to John Walker:

'My fate drives me from one extreme to another. A few months ago the whole southern hemisphere was hardly big enough for me, and now I am going to be confined within the limits of Greenwich Hospital, which are far too small for an active mind like mine. I must confess it a fine retreat and a pretty income, but whether I can bring myself to like ease and retirement time will show.'

The published account of the *Endeavour's* voyage, although a best-seller, had been disastrous in several ways. Hawkesworth, the editor, had combined the journals of Cook and Banks and added his own particular 'literary' flavour; and the result had been a pompous, often inaccurate work which gave the public a largely false picture of the voyage and of the places and peoples met with. With time on his hands Cook decided to write his own account of the second voyage, based on his journal. With some discreet editorial help from Canon Douglas, of Windsor, it emerged as a simple, straightforward narrative, and when it was eventually published in 1777 the whole edition sold out on the first day.

While Cook was thus engaged the coming voyage of the *Resolution* prompted a revival of the old question whether there existed a passage

from the north Atlantic to the north Pacific around the top of America. Something like fifty attempts, dating back to Cabot's in 1497, had already been made to find this, and an offer by Parliament of a reward of £20,000 for the man who did still stood. In 1742 Vitus Bering, a Swede in the Russian Navy, had proved the existence of a strait separating the north-western tip of America from Asia; and it was now suggested that the job should be tackled simultaneously from both sides—by the *Resolution* from the west through Bering Strait, and by another ship from the east through Baffin Bay—in the hope that at some point both expeditions might meet. The Admiralty approved. As the *Adventure* was not again available it was decided to buy another consort for the *Resolution*. Cook was called in to advise, and on his recommendation another Whitby-built collier, the *Diligence*, two hundred and ninety-eight tons, was acquired, refitted and re-named the *Discovery*. The approach through Baffin's Bay was to be made by the armed brig *Lyon*, with Cook's old comrade Richard Pickersgill in command.

The obvious man to command the *Resolution* was, of course, Cook himself, but out of respect for his retirement his name was carefully avoided. Instead, early in February 1776 Lord Sandwich gave a dinner party with Palliser, Phillip Stephens (Secretary to the Admiralty) and Cook himself as guests. Its ostensible purpose was to ask Cook's advice about the appointment; its real one was the hope that he might volunteer his own

services. If Cook saw the trap he fell a willing victim to it, and two days later he was officially appointed to command the expedition, with Charles Clerke as captain of the *Discovery*.

The *Revolution*'s complement was a hundred and twelve, the *Discovery*'s seventy. As his first lieutenant Cook had John Gore, veteran of the *Dolphin* and *Endeavour* voyages. His second was James King, a young officer of some brilliance who combined practical seamanship with a flair for astronomy, and his third was John Williamson. His master, although aged only twenty-two was already known as a brilliant navigator; his name William Bligh. Cook's experience of the Forsters had made him wary of professional botanists, and this time the work was entrusted to the ship's surgeon William Anderson, who on the second voyage had proved himself a skilled naturalist and ethnologist. The official artist was John Webber, aged twenty-four, the son of a Swiss sculptor living in London, and among others with some skill as draughtsmen were midshipman Henry Roberts, who redrew most of Bligh's charts for publication, and James Cleveley, carpenter, a younger brother of John Cleveley, a noted marine artist. Clerke's first lieutenant was James Burney, his second John Rickman. His master was Thomas Edgar, and his midshipmen included George Vancouver. On the *Discovery* graphic work was entrusted to the surgeon's mate, William Ellis, a graduate of Cambridge and St

Far left John Webber, official artist on the third voyage. By J. D. Mottet, from a miniature

Centre left John Montagu, 4th Earl of Sandwich, by Thomas Gainsborough. As First Lord of the Admiralty he was mainly responsible for Cook undertaking his third voyage

Above Christmas Harbour, Kerguelen's Land, a bleak, treeless waste which Cook's men appropriately called the Island of Desolation. The drawing is by William Ellis, surgeon's second mate on the *Discovery*

Left Marine dipping needle, or inclinometer, an instrument for measuring the variations of the world's magnetic field. Cook and his astronomers were instructed to use these instruments daily. This one was probably used by Cook on his third voyage

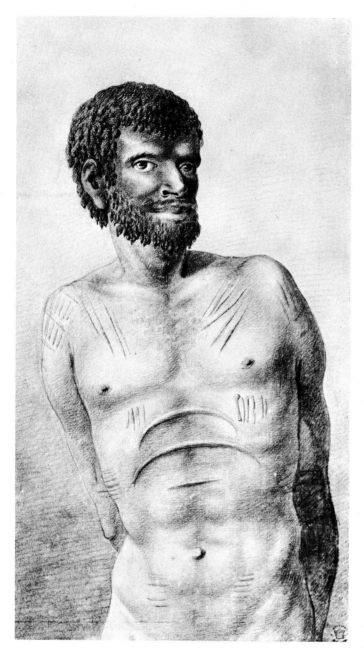

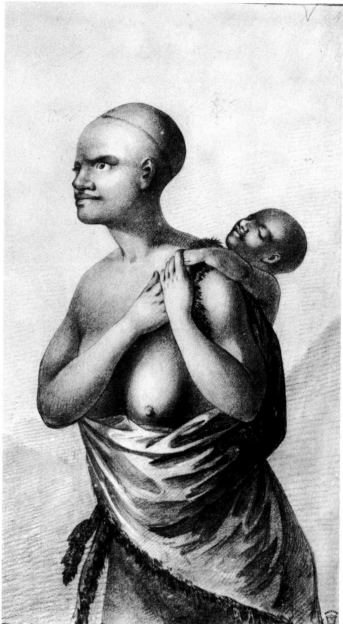

Far left A man of Van Diemen's Land, by John Webber. This is the first known portrait of a Tasmanian native. Contact with whites was disastrous, and by the 1880s the race was extinct

Left Webber's portrait of a woman of Van Diemen's Land. The men went naked and the women wore only a kangaroo-skin

Bottom left Hunting sea-lions in the Arctic. A water-colour sketch by Webber which he developed later into an oil-painting for the Admiralty

Above A possum of Van Diemen's Land. An anatomically incorrect engraving from Webber's original drawing which was published in the official account of the third voyage

Bart's, who had considerable skill as an amateur artist; and David Nelson, a young gardener from Kew, went along to collect plants for Banks. William Bayly, astronomer aboard the *Adventure*, sailed this time in the *Discovery*, but because of the skill of Cook and King the Board of Longitude decided there was no need to send one in the *Resolution*. The expedition included altogether twenty-three who had sailed previously with Cook, of whom six had been on both voyages. These included Clerke, William Peckover (gunner) and Samuel Gibson, now a sergeant of marines.

A son named Hugh, after Palliser, was born to Mrs Cook on 23rd May. Four weeks later Cook said goodbye to his family for what was to be the last time, and by the end of June the *Resolution* had joined the *Discovery* at Plymouth. Here a variety of livestock—a personal gift from the king—including cattle, sheep, goats and pigs were taken aboard for distribution in the South Sea islands. Here too Omai joined the *Resolution* so laden down with presents, including a custom-made suit of armour, that he could barely move in his cabin. Departure was delayed for some time by the non-appearance of Clerke. He had guaranteed the debts of his brother, Captain Sir John Clerke, RN, who had sailed for the East Indies without settling them, and was being dunned by creditors. On instructions from the Admiralty the *Resolution* sailed alone on 12th July. Eventually Clerke managed to extricate himself after a period in a debtors' prison, and the *Discovery* put to sea on 1st August.

The *Resolution*'s first and only stop on the way south was at Tenerife, to take on water, wine, and fodder for the livestock. The shipwrights had done a poor job, and in the hot weather of the tropics her seams opened and she began to leak badly in all her upper works, including her main deck. 'There was hardly a man who could lie dry in his bed,' Cook wrote. The officers were driven out of their cabins, and several sails stored in the sail-room were ruined before they could be dried out.

At Cape Town, which was reached on 17th October, Cook personally supervised the recaulking. The stock were put ashore to graze, and some sheep were stolen. Cook replaced them with Cape sheep, and for good measure bought some horses and rabbits. Omai was delighted and willingly gave up his cabin to stable four of the horses. 'Nothing is now wanting but a few females of our own species to make the *Resolution* a complete Ark', Cook wrote to Lord Sandwich. With Gore and Omai as his companions Anderson spent five days botanizing in the interior. The *Discovery* arrived on 10th November, leaking as badly as the *Resolution*. She was soon patched up, and on 1st December the ships sailed in company—'to return to our old trade of exploring', as Clerke wrote to Banks.

Twelve days out several small islands first reported by the French navigator Marion du Fresne were seen. Cook called them the Prince Edward Group, but spent little time examining them. Kerguelen's Land, for which search had been made without success on the second voyage, was located on 24th December, and proved to be a cluster of islands, bleak, rocky and treeless, inhabited by seals and multitudes of penguins. Next morning the ships anchored in a sheltered bay which Cook called Christmas Harbour. Fortunately there was ample grass for the stock; even so several cattle and goats died.

Through January 1777 the two ships sailed almost due east pushed along by the fierce westerlies of the 'roaring forties'. On the 24th the south coast of Van Diemen's Land came into sight, and two days later the ships anchored in Adventure Bay to take on wood and water and to gather fodder for the livestock. During Furneaux's visit no natives had appeared. This time they were less shy, and a sort of precarious friendship with them was established. Cook, who thought Van Diemen's Land part of the mainland, was surprised that they differed so greatly from the natives of New Holland. Anderson found them 'mild and cheerful, without reserve or jealousy of strangers', but they seemed to him neither particularly enterprising nor intelligent. His assistant, David Samwell, considered the women 'the ugliest creatures that can be imagined in human shape'. Certainly they were a primitive race. The women wore a piece of kangaroo skin around their shoulders to carry infants on their backs; otherwise both sexes went naked. The men bedaubed themselves with red clay, and their only ornamentation consisted of raised weals on their bodies. The women in general shaved their heads. Their huts were miserable, they had few weapons, no canoes were seen, they seemed not to understand the purpose of fish-hooks, and they appeared to live almost entirely on shellfish. The hills around Adventure Bay (which is, in fact, on Bruny Island) were thickly wooded, with eucalypts predominating. The only

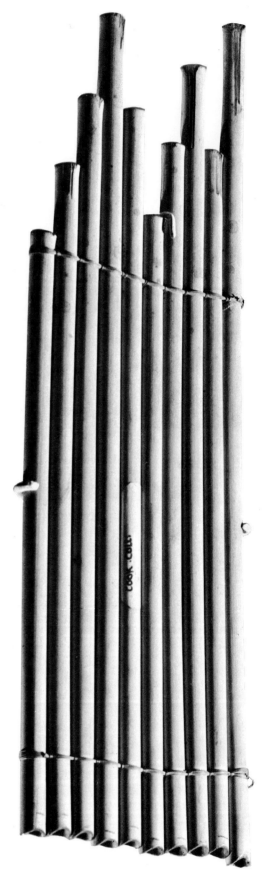

Above Reed pipes from Tonga, one of the musical instruments used at the entertainments provided for Cook and his men. This set was given to Cook as a present and taken home by him

Right Fighting club from Tonga, about five feet long. The intricately carved design incorporates human figures and birds

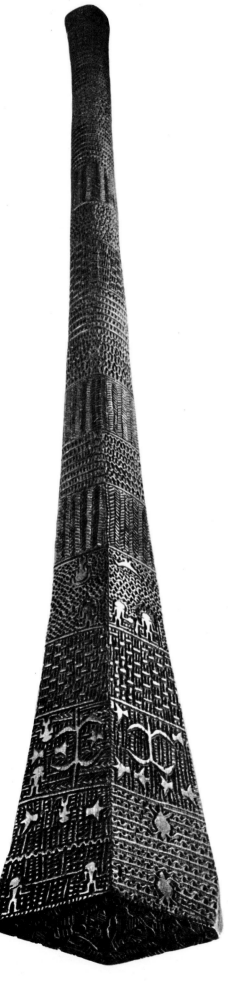

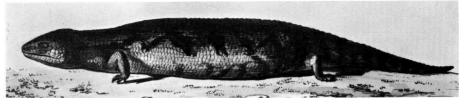

Top A blue-tongued lizard of Adventure Bay, Van Diemen's Land, by Webber. These are also common on the Australian mainland

Centre William Ellis caught much of the spectacular scenic quality of Tahiti in this view up the valley from Matavai Bay. It was this river which provided fresh water for Cook's and other visiting ships

Above The river at Vaitepiha Bay, on the south-east coast of Tahiti, by Ellis. Today a causeway crosses it to the village of Tautira, where Robert Louis Stevenson lived for some months

animal seen was 'a sort of opossum', which was shot, but obviously there were kangaroos as well. Fish were plentiful and each netting produced more than enough to feed all hands. Anderson found several new species of birds, some of which Webber drew. There were many snakes and large lizards, not to mention mosquitoes, flies and 'a large black ant whose bite is almost intolerable for the short time it lasts', obviously the present-day Australian 'bull-dog ant'.

After four days the ships sailed east for New Zealand, and on 12th February they reached the usual anchorage in Queen Charlotte's Sound. Many natives paddled alongside in canoes, but few would venture aboard. Cook supposed they were afraid he had come to avenge the massacre of the *Adventure*'s boat crew, and through Omai he assured them this was not so. After that they became more friendly, and within a few days so many families had moved in that a whole series of villages sprang up on the shores of the cove. Among the visitors

was a chief named Kahura, a fierce and dominating man who seemed 'more feared than beloved' by the other natives. It was he who had instigated the attack on the *Adventure*'s men, and he who had struck the first blow. According to the Maori code Cook was entitled to kill him, and they were bewildered when he declined to do so. So was Omai. 'If a man kills another in England he is hanged for it,' he pointed out. 'This man has killed ten, and yet you will not kill him, though a great many of his countrymen desire it.' Omai added darkly that he would willingly do the job himself, but his threat was not carried out. Instead, Kahura sat for a portrait by Webber.

Cook was delighted to find that cabbages, onions, leeks, parsley, radishes and a few potatoes he had planted were still growing, and to learn that pigs and poultry had multiplied and were running wild in the woods. It was his hope that once ample meat was available the Maoris might turn from cannibalism.

Top left A Maori encampment at Queen Charlotte's Sound, with the *Resolution* and *Discovery* in the background. By Webber

Left Cook and his officers watch a human sacrifice in Tahiti. These were rare, and the victims were usually criminals killed while asleep

Above The village at Waimea, on the island of Kauai, in the Hawaiian group. Drawn by Webber

Right An unfinished drawing by Webber of Hawaiian canoes with masked paddlers. The masks were made of gourds and probably played a ritual part in worship of god Lono, whom the islanders identified with Cook

From his own stock he turned loose a male and a female goat, a boar and a sow, after having extracted a promise from the natives that they would not be killed.

The ships stayed a fortnight, and when they sailed on 25th February there were two Maoris aboard the *Resolution*—Te Weherua, aged about eighteen, the son of a chief, and his boy servant Koa. Cook was reluctant to take them and explained that they would probably never have a chance to return, but this did not daunt them.

From New Zealand a course was set north-east for Tahiti, where Cook meant to land most of his remaining stock, but persistent headwinds made progress slow. Late in March several islands of what is now the Cook Group were discovered, including Mangaia and Atiu. Both were completely circled by reefs, which made a landing almost impossible. Finally a party which included Burney, Anderson and Omai managed to get ashore on Atiu by going as far as the reef in a ship's

boat and then transferring to a canoe. The natives, who spoke a Polynesian dialect which Omai understood, were friendly and received their visitors with great courtesy. Presents were exchanged but there was no point in trading as it would have been impossible to get the goods off. On the island Omai met three Tahitians, the survivors of twenty whose canoe had been driven off-course by a gale while on a routine voyage from Tahiti to Raiatea. They were so happy on Atiu that they declined an offer to be taken back to Tahiti.

Fresh fodder for the livestock was urgently needed, and Cook decided to turn west for the Friendly Islands rather than continue to battle against the easterlies which blocked his way to Tahiti. The group came in sight on 28th April, and next day anchor was dropped off Mango, a small island near Nomuka. The Tongans welcomed the white men with great joy. They were as charming and friendly as ever, and Cook was treated as a great chief. Hitherto he had been a man of strong

and single purpose; now his behaviour became so uncharacteristic that historians still find it hard to excuse or even explain. Certainly time was running short, but at a pinch he could still have reached Bering Strait during the late summer. But instead valuable time was spent in pleasant but generally pointless cruising through the archipelago, with long stops at Eua, Tongatabu, Nomuka and in the Haapai Group. The natives entertained their visitors with singing, dancing, wrestling and boxing matches (in which the women took part) and mock fights. In return Cook treated them to a fireworks display and had his marines drilled. Natives who were caught thieving were flogged and otherwise punished—one had a cross cut on his arm with a knife— and on occasions hostages were held until stolen articles had been returned. In fairness to Cook, any of his own men who offended against natives were dealt with equally severely. Cook and Omai were not only invited to attend the secret initiation of a chief's son, but actually took part in the ceremony, stripped to the waist with their hair streaming loose around their shoulders. Fraternisation reached such a point that some Tongan girls virtually lived aboard the ships, and moved with them from island to island.

By 25th June Cook's conscience was troubling him. But an eclipse of the sun, scheduled for 5th July, provided a good excuse to linger on, and in fact another fortnight passed after that before a final move was made. Although

this was strange enough it was by no means all. Cook had learned that two extensive groups of islands lay within a few days' easy sail—Fiji to the north-west, a high rich country peopled by numerous 'cannibals, brave, savage and cruel'; and Samoa, whose people had much in common with the Tongans, to the north-east. The reports were confirmed many times over and Cook could have been in no doubt about them for there were men from both island groups actually on Tongatabu. Yet to the barely-concealed amazement of those who had experienced his insatiable curiosity he made no attempt to explore either group; nor did he attempt to explain the omission in his journal. Perhaps the reason is not so hard to find. After all, he was almost forty-eight, and for nine years he had driven himself hard, at times almost to the limit of human endurance.

After an idyllic twelve weeks among the Friendly Islanders the *Resolution* and *Discovery* sailed for Tahiti on 17th July. Three weeks later they passed Tubuai, one of the most southerly of what are now the Austral Islands. Natives came out in canoes and urged the visitors to go ashore, an invitation which Cook would normally never have refused. But on this occasion, he wrote, he 'did not think it proper to lose the advantage of a fair wind for the sake of examining an island that appeared of little consequence', and the ships sailed on.

Tahiti came into sight on 11th August, and next day anchors were dropped in Vaitepiha Bay. As soon as

Top left The *Resolution* at anchor in Nootka Sound, Vancouver Island. By Webber

Far left Ceremonial cloak from Hawaii, of net work with red and yellow feathers, which were sacred colours knotted into the mesh. Taken back by Webber

Centre left A woven basketry hat surmounted by four cylinders, from Nootka Sound

Bottom left Ceremonial helmet worn by Hawaiian chiefs, covered with red and yellow feathers and shaped like an ancient Greek helmet. Taken back by Webber

Right A tattooed Hawaiian, by Webber

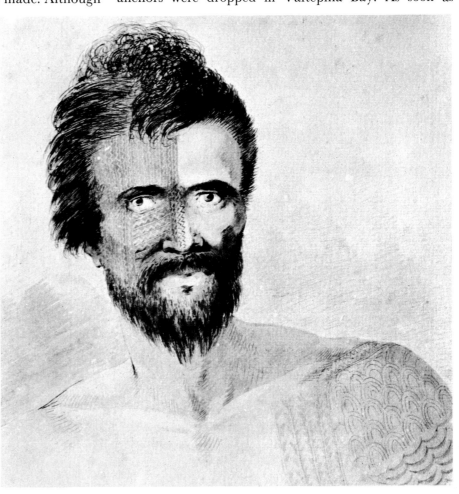

word reached shore that a new supply of red feathers had been brought the natives swarmed out in their canoes to trade hogs and fruit. Twelve days later the ships moved to Matavai Bay, where they were welcomed by Tu and 'a prodigious crowd'. Impressed by Omai's European clothes and sophisticated manner and by the many presents he had brought back, Tu and other leading natives urged him to stay in Tahiti. But Omai preferred the company of common people—'refugees and strangers', as Cook called them—and said he would rather return to Huahine. Most of the livestock were landed, and Cook and Clerke created a sensation when they galloped over the Matavai plain on horseback. The natives were astounded, and Cook was sure it gave them 'a better idea of the greatness of other nations than all the other things put together'.

Although both crews were in their usual good health Cook himself was suffering from rheumatic pains in the side and leg. Tu sent his mother, three sisters and eight other women aboard the *Resolution*, and in relays they massaged the affected spots so skilfully that after a day the pains disappeared. However, there was to be no such easy relief for Clerke or Anderson. Both had developed consumption—Clerke possibly as a result of his imprisonment in London—and, in doubt whether they would survive the rigours of an Arctic winter, they discussed the possibility of resigning their positions and settling in Tahiti. But Clerke found various excuses, and in the end nothing was said or done.

At Cook's request Tu sat for Webber, and when he asked the reason Cook explained that he meant to keep the picture as a permanent reminder of the Tahitian chief and his friendship. The idea so charmed Tu that he asked for a portrait of Cook in return. With some persuasion Cook agreed to sit, and the portrait when completed was framed and fitted into a box with lock and key. In later years Tu brought it out proudly to show to the captains of other visiting ships, and it still

Above The ships at anchor in Nootka Sound, also called King George's Sound. The observatory tents were erected on what was called Astronomers' Rock. By Ellis

Below Webber's impression of a woman of Nootka Sound. The decorated hat and fringed cloak were typical

Top right Interior of a house at Nootka Sound, by Webber. These houses were long and shared by several families. Cook was unable to discover the significance of the carved idols

Right A ceremonial tomahawk of Nootka Sound. It comprises a stone blade attached to a carved wooden handle into which human hair has been inserted. Collected by Webber

existed as late as 1792 when Bligh visited Tahiti on his second breadfruit voyage.

Although the island of Moorea lay only twelve miles from Tahiti Cook had never visited it, mainly because he understood it had no harbours. Now he decided to do so, and on 30th September the *Resolution* and *Discovery* crossed the narrow strait. To Cook's surprise he found two good harbours on the north side—Tareu (now generally called Papetoai) and Paopao. The latter is still known as Cook's Bay, though in fact Tareu was the one he chose. The visit was not altogether happy. A goat was stolen, and Cook chose to make a major issue of it. He marched across the island with a large armed party, and on his orders several houses and canoes were burned. Next day he let it be known that he would destroy every canoe on the island, and in fact about a dozen had been burned or hacked to bits before the goat was returned.

From Moorea the ships moved on to Huahine. Cook asked for some land for Omai and was told with great courtesy that as the whole island was his he could take whatever part of it he pleased. A site was chosen about two hundred yards square, carpenters from both ships built a small house on it, and a garden was planted with vegetables and fruit. Among the numerous presents Omai brought ashore were a horse, a mare, a goat, a boar and a sow, a musket, a fowling piece, pistols and a supply of powder and shot. The young Maoris Te Weherua and Koa remained with him, and with his brother, sister and brother-in-law and some servants he had brought from Tahiti his household numbered ten.

At Huahine the usual petty thieving took a serious turn when a sextant disappeared. It was recovered and the thief, a native of Bora Bora, apprehended. Because of his insolence Cook punished him 'with greater severity' than he had ever punished a man before. In fact, so Clerke records, the unfortunate fellow's ears were cut off and he was then turned loose. In revenge

he destroyed part of Omai's garden and boasted that he would kill him and burn down his house as soon as the white men left. Cook had him seized again and put in irons, intending to return him to Bora Bora, but he escaped and stayed in hiding until the ships sailed.

At Raiatea there was trouble of a different kind. Two of the *Discovery*'s crew deserted, and to force the natives to find and return them Cook followed his now familiar practice of seizing hostages. This time they were a son, a daughter and a son-in-law of the chief of the island. The daughter, Poetua, was such a beauty that Webber sketched her and on his return to England developed this into a portrait in oils. The Raiateans planned in retaliation to seize Clerke and Gore, but the plot was given away by a girl who had accompanied the *Resolution* from Huahine. Eventually the deserters were found hiding on a small atoll and Cook confined them in irons until the ships sailed on 7th December. There was a brief visit to Bora Bora, and next day a course was set almost due north into unknown waters.

The equator was crossed on 22nd December, and two days later a barren, uninhabited island was found. Cook named it Christmas Island, and as fish and turtle were plentiful he decided to stay a few days for the sake of his men. On the 30th Cook, Bayly and King went ashore to observe an eclipse of the sun, but Clerke was too ill to accompany them. Two men from the *Resolution* managed to lose themselves for a day, and when found

Above Interior of a winter house at Unalaska, an island of the Aleutians, by Webber. These were covered with turf, and the only access was through a hole in the roof, which also served as a chimney

Left Carved wooden warrior's staff with totemic emblems from the north-west American coast. The warrior may have belonged to the wolf clan. The hair decorating the human masks was often taken from an enemy's scalp, and was believed to possess supernatural power

Top right A view in Unalaska, by Webber

Right A figure from Nootka Sound, taken to Europe by Webber

Far right A man of Sandwich (Prince William) Sound, Alaska. By Webber

were suffering severely from thirst. Yams, coconuts and melons were planted for the benefit of later visitors and on 2nd January 1778 the voyage was resumed.

On 18th January two high islands were seen ahead. In an attempt to render their native names Cook called them Atoui and Eneeheeou; on modern maps they appear as Kauai and Niihau. Natives came out from Kauai in canoes, but although friendly enough they could not be coaxed on board. In appearance they were like Tahitians but darker, and their language was so similar as to leave no doubt that they came of common stock. Cook, who had never expected to find Polynesians so far north, was lost in wonder. To his own certain knowledge they peopled an area of over one thousand two hundred leagues north to south and one thousand six hundred and sixty leagues east to west—nearly equal to all Africa, as Clerke pointed out. 'How,' Cook asked, 'shall we account for this nation spreading itself so far over this vast ocean?', and he could find no answer.

Trouble came soon enough. Three boats were sent off to look for a landing place and water, and as one of them neared the shore the natives 'pressed so thick about it' that Williamson, who was in charge of the party, fired and shot one dead. Knowing how angry his commander would be he failed to report the incident, and Cook learned of it only after they had left the islands. But the power of the white strangers had been demonstrated and had left its imprint. Next day when Cook went

ashore a crowd of several hundreds 'fell flat on their faces'—a gesture of respect and submission usually reserved for kings—and stayed so until he signed to them to rise. Again, as he walked with Anderson and Webber to a village called Waimea, people all along the route prostrated themselves as he passed; and a week later when he went ashore on Niihau he was accorded the same honour.

Cook was deeply impressed by the natives and their way of life. He found them 'an open, candid, active people', honest in their dealings and less given to thieving than most Polynesians. Samwell conceded that the young women were 'in general exceeding beautiful', but added censoriously that they had no more sense of modesty than the Tahitian girls, and brazenly tried to lure the strangers into their houses. Cook considered the natives the best swimmers he had ever seen—even infants, he noted, were completely at home in the water —and Clerke concurred. Their canoes, Clerke wrote, were inferior to none but those of the Friendly Islands, which were probably the best in the world; and they were also able to travel through the water at great speed on boards, about eight feet long, on which they lay prone, paddling with their hands and steering with their feet. They tattooed themselves sparingly, and both sexes went naked from the waist up. Chiefs and a few people of consequence wore cloaks of red and yellow feathers with caps of the same material, shaped like

Cook was persuaded by Joseph Banks to sit for this portrait by Nathaniel Dance in 1776, soon before he left England on his final voyage. The original is in the National Maritime Museum, Greenwich

Left The ships at anchor in Snug Corner, Prince William Sound, Alaska, with Eskimos in canoes and kayaks. By Ellis

The *Resolution* and *Discovery*
in danger of being trapped in the ice
north of Bering Strait. Webber later
developed this drawing into a
spectacular aquatint

ancient Greek helmets. So high a value was set on these
capes and helmets that Cook could not obtain any.
'However, some were got,' he added, but did not say
how or by whom. Their cloth was the same as Tahitian
tapa, but glazed for rainproofing and printed in a
'pretty and pleasing' variety of colours and designs.
Their huts were not scattered as on other islands but
built close together to form villages. They were well-
made, shaped 'like corn stacks', and their floors were
covered with hay and sleeping mats. Their main weapons
were spears and lances and 'a sort of dagger' about a
foot and a half long, but they did not seem a warlike
people. Although the islands were not as fertile as some
in the Pacific they grew the same fruits and vegetables,
and as elsewhere fish, hogs and poultry were abundant.
Cook left three goats, a boar and a sow in the hope that
they would breed, and also some vegetable seeds.

To the east another large island could be seen which
the natives called Oahu, but Cook lacked time to
explore it. He was not to know that beyond the south-
eastern horizon lay five other islands, including the
largest of them all. In gratitude to his patron he named
the group the Sandwich Islands. The name survived
into the nineteenth century, but today they are officially
known as the Hawaiian Islands.

The ships were on their way again on 2nd February,
heading north-west to reach the west coast of the
American continent, or as Cook called it 'New Albion'.
Five days later, as they battled against squally north-
west winds, land was sighted ahead in latitude 44°33'
north, a little more than halfway up the coast of the
present State of Oregon. It was of moderate height and
thickly wooded; and it formed a point which Cook, for
obvious reasons, named Cape Foul Weather. The name
has stuck. A few days later the wind veered favourably,
and the ships were able to resume their voyage northward.
Cook was looking for the Strait of Juan de Fuca which
appeared on some charts, but saw nothing like it and

An impression by Ellis of the exterior of a winter house at Unalaska, with the top of a notched log, used as a ladder, emerging from the entrance

convinced himself it did not exist. In fact he was wrong, for he passed it in the night. Had he found and sailed up this strait he may well have discovered the site of the present city of Vancouver.

Weather drove the ships far out to sea and a week passed before land was seen again. It comprised snow-covered mountains intersecting thickly-wooded valleys, and, having missed the Strait of Juan de Fuca, Cook assumed wrongly it was part of the mainland. Both ships, particularly the *Resolution*, were in need of repair, and a good anchorage was found in a deep, sheltered inlet with a central island which Cook named after Bligh. Natives who came out in canoes seemed mild and inoffensive, and showed no fear of the visitors. They called the place Nootka; Cook's alternative name—King George's Sound—appears on few modern maps. Knives, chisels, nails and anything iron were in keen demand and were traded for skins—bear, wolf, fox, raccoon, polecat, martin and sea-beaver; and Cook had

no doubt that enterprising traders could establish a profitable market. Wood and watering parties went ashore, and carpenters and blacksmiths set to work on the ships. The *Resolution*'s mizzen mast was so badly strained that a new one was cut, personally chosen by Cook. After three weeks of continuous rain the weather cleared, and Cook set out to explore and chart the sound. With rare exceptions he was received with great courtesy at the villages he visited.

In spite of the friendliness of the natives the visitors found little to admire in them. They were commonly a silent and grave people, short and stocky in build, with broad, flat faces, and high cheek-bones. Both sexes daubed themselves liberally with black, red and white ochre mixed with oil and they stank inordinately. Certainly, Cook wrote, they had 'no pretensions to being called beauties'. Their clothes, mostly made from furs, included a cloak like a 'round dish cover' with a hole in the centre just big enough for the head to pass

Below View of Adventure Bay, Van Diemen's Land, where Cook stayed briefly during his third voyage. The artist is William Ellis, surgeon's second mate aboard the *Discovery*

Bottom Maoris and white men at Queen Charlotte's Sound, New Zealand, during Cook's third voyage. Aquatint by John Webber

Below This picture by John Cleveley is an interesting example of how errors creep in when an artist has not been on the spot. It is supposed to represent the *Resolution* and *Discovery* in Queen Charlotte's Sound, New Zealand. But coconut trees do not grow in New Zealand, the natives seen are in Tahitian dress, and the canoe with raised sail is Tongan. The scene appears to represent Matavai Bay, Tahiti

Bottom Maoris inside a hippah, or native village, near Queen Charlotte's Sound, New Zealand. By John Webber

through, and they wore straw hats like inverted flower-pots. Their houses were of timber, up to a hundred and fifty feet long and divided into family apartments, and in most of them were large, rudely-carved wooden images, the significance of which the visitors were unable to learn. Inside, Cook wrote, the houses were 'as filthy as hog-sties' and reeked of fish, oil and smoke. They were hunters and fishermen, with well-made dugout canoes up to forty feet long, and their main weapons were bows and arrows, slings, spears and tomahawks. The tomahawks were unique in Cook's experience. They were of stone, with wooden handles carved to represent human heads and necks and decorated with human hair; and the blades looked like 'enormous large tongues'.

During almost four weeks at Nootka Sound the only unpleasantness was occasional petty thieving, and when the ships sailed on 25th April friendly natives in their canoes escorted them to the entrance.

Heading north-west the ships groped their way along a rugged and weather-beaten coast. Cook named as he went—Cape and Mount Edgcumbe, the Bay of Islands, Cross Sound, Cape and Mount Fairweather, Mount St Elias. They were now off Alaska, and the coastline trended sharply west. The *Resolution* was in a bad way again, leaking freely, and Cook looked for and found a protected harbour. Here she was heeled over and unsheathed and her gaping seams, in which scarcely

a strand of oakum remained, were recaulked. Cook called the anchorage Sandwich Sound, but later it was altered to Prince William's Sound. They stayed only long enough for the carpenters to do their work; then they were on their way again.

A wide inlet, trending north-east, suggested to some of the officers that this might be the entrance to a north-west passage. Cook was dubious but agreed to explore it, and several valuable days were spent sailing up its two hundred miles. Then they found themselves hemmed in on all sides by snow-topped mountains and were obliged to turn back. Off the mainland coast again they sailed south-west along the length of the Alaskan peninsula until it broke up into a chain of islands, the Aleutians. There was a brief stop at one of these, Unalaska; then the ships sailed up the far side of the long peninsula and so into the Bering Sea. The country they saw was wild and inhospitable, its fog-bound coast deeply indented and strewn with rocks and shoals. At Cape Newenham on the Alaskan mainland Williamson went ashore, climbed a hill and took possession of the country in the name of King George III.

On 3rd August Cook recorded with regret the death of William Anderson, after an illness of twelve months. 'He was a sensible young man', he wrote, 'an agreeable companion, well skilled in his profession, and he had acquired much knowledge in other sciences'. No doubt Clerke wished both of them had stayed in Tahiti.

Below French 18th century wallpaper with design based on themes from Cook's voyages. It comprised twenty sections, of which eleven are shown here, and was designed by J. C. Charvet for Joseph Dufour, of Mâcon, who exhibited it in 1806. An emphasis on ideas of classical Greece is perhaps not so ridiculous if the physical build, bearing, manners and clothing of Polynesians of Cook's time are considered

Above Apart from his landscape
work Ellis was an accomplished
natural history draughtsman. This
drawing of the Crested Auklet
(*Aethia cristatella*) was made off the
Alaskan coast

Webber's impression of natives
dancing at Tongatabu (Tonga). The
friendliness of the natives and lavish
entertainments of this kind tempted
Cook to linger there on his third
voyage

Anderson willed his plants and curiosities to Joseph
Banks, and his papers to relatives in Scotland.

The western extremity of Alaska, which Cook called
Cape Prince of Wales, was reached on 8th August. The
ships crossed Bering Strait to the Asian mainland, and
anchored briefly off a small village, inhabited by 'long-
visaged, stout-made' people of Mongol type. They
doffed their caps and bowed low when Cook landed,
but remained suspicious and little contact was made.

On their way north through the strait the ships
crossed the Arctic Circle. It was now mid-August. The
cold was intense, the weather was bad and worsening,
the short summer was almost over, and within a few
days the ships were virtually locked in a vast field of
pack-ice which stretched to infinity. Baffin Bay lay only
a few hundred miles to the east, but it may as well have
been a million miles. As Cook was a year behind
schedule the question of linking up with an expedition
from the east did not arise; in any case, although he was
not to know it, the attempt had long since been abandoned and Pickersgill was in disgrace, discharged from

the Navy for drunkenness. For a week or more Cook
conscientiously probed this way and that, but the ice
was impenetrable. Finally he gave up and turned back,
planning to winter in the Sandwich Islands and try
again next summer.

The *Resolution* was once more in bad shape, and three
weeks were spent in Unalaska while the carpenters
worked on her. Cook met several Russian traders who
knew the area well and despite language difficulties they
were able to fill in several blanks on his charts. During
their months around the Alaskan coast the ships had
often been visited by Eskimos in their kayaks, eager to
trade furs for tobacco. Now Cook was able to get to
know them better, and he found them scrupulously
honest and 'the most peaceable, inoffensive people' he
had ever met. They were small, thick-set and good-
looking, and as they did not paint themselves like the
Nootka Sound natives they were personally cleaner.
In summer they lived in timber houses. Their winter
residences, however, were oval-shaped, about twenty-
four feet long, framed of wood and whale ribs, and

For a while Matavai Bay, Tahiti, was the most painted spot in the Pacific. Unlike most, this view by William Ellis was made from Point Venus, where Cook had his camp, looking towards One Tree Hill

covered with thick sods of earth, to which the only entry was a hole in the top. From the outside they looked 'like dung-hills', Cook wrote, and inside they were 'lousy and filthy'.

In violent weather two days out from Unalaska the main tack of the *Discovery* broke, killing one man and injuring three. Except for this mishap the voyage south was uneventful.

Maui, the second largest of the Sandwich Islands, was sighted on 26th November. Natives who came out to trade welcomed the newcomers warmly but without surprise, and Cook assumed rightly that word of their previous visit had spread through the islands. Among those who came aboard was an old man who, by the deference shown him, was assumed to be a chief. In fact, as they were to learn later, he was Kalaniopu, king of Hawaii, and without doubt the object of his visit was to sum up the white men and particularly Cook.

Hawaii itself was seen four days later, and Cook was astonished to find that its twin peaks, Mauna Kea and Mauna Loa, which rise to almost fourteen thousand feet, were covered with snow. For more than a fortnight the ships ranged slowly along the north coast looking for an anchorage. Another fortnight was spent trying to get to windward of the island, and yet another eleven days went by before the ships managed to round the south point. Every day scores of canoes came out carrying, as Cook put it succinctly, 'hogs and women', the latter 'more ready to bestow their favours' than any he had ever known. Even so the crews were impatient to get ashore, and for the first time Cook found himself obliged to cope with seething discontent in the forecastle. He did so tolerantly and well.

Eventually on 16th January 1779 a possible anchorage was seen. Bligh was sent to examine it, and returned with a good report. The bay was called Kealakekua, and on its shores were two villages—Kekua, where good water was to be got, and Kavarua. When the ships anchored next morning the reception was overwhelming. According to King's estimate at least fifteen hundred canoes containing nine thousand natives came out to welcome them. Many more paddled out on surfboards;

hundreds, mainly young women and boys, swam around the ships 'like shoals of fish'; and thousands more lined the foreshores of the bay. The situation on board the *Resolution* threatened to get out of hand until Palea, a young chief, and Koa, a high priest, arrived and restored order. Cook was treated with great deference, and Koa ceremoniously wrapped him in a piece of red cloth which he had brought with other gifts. In the afternoon Cook, King and several others were escorted ashore with equal ceremony. The assembled thousands prostrated themselves, and priests greeted Cook with speeches of submission in which the word 'Lono' was frequently repeated. From the beach they were led to a *heiau*, or sacred place, where there were many idols, and here they took part in 'a long and tiresome ceremony' the nature of which they did not understand. It was clear enough that in Hawaiian eyes Cook was a great king; in fact, it went much further than that. King wrote that the homage they paid him 'seemed to approach to adoration' and he was right, for the purpose of the ceremony was to acknowledge Cook as an incarnation of Lono, the god of peace, happiness and agriculture, whose return to the island in human form had been predicted, and to command the people to worship him as such.

Although unaware that he had been deified Cook realized that it was up to him to maintain appearances, and when watering parties went ashore next morning the marines who accompanied them were in full regimentals and under strict orders to behave in a soldierly manner. An observatory and marquees were erected near Kekua, and Palea kept the curious hordes away by the simple process of declaring the area *tabu*. Whenever Cook landed priests were there to greet him and pay homage, and minor chiefs who came to his marquee laden with presents behaved in great awe of him. With special permission a few men ventured within the area, but the women resisted all persuasions to do so, saying that if they did they would be killed.

On 24th January there was a remarkable change. No canoes came out, and the people kept close to their houses. Cook feared that he had offended in some way, and was relieved to learn that the ban on intercourse was merely temporary and had been imposed because of the imminent arrival of the king. Kalaniopu appeared next day. In contrast to his earlier unofficial appearance he was accompanied this time by a glittering retinue and brought many gifts. He was 'a tall, thin old man, apparently more worn out with debauching than with age', Burney wrote, but although his limbs trembled he carried himself upright and with regal dignity. He wore a magnificent cloak of red and yellow feathers and a helmet of the same material, and these he took off and put on Cook. Many other gifts including six more cloaks were placed at Cook's feet, and he and the king exchanged names in token of friendship. Later Cook

Above The war god Kukailimoku, a carved wooden figure from a temple in Hawaii

Right Kukailimoku, the Hawaiian god of war. Over a basketry frame fine mesh was drawn, into which red and yellow feathers were knotted. The eyes are of pearl-shell, and the mouth is fitted with polished dogs' teeth

took Kalaniopu and some others aboard the *Resolution* and distributed many presents in return.

For awhile fraternisation on the island was complete. Men off duty roamed the countryside often alone and unarmed and were treated everywhere as honoured guests. There were dancing, wrestling and boxing matches for the entertainment of the visitors, and Cook responded with a fireworks display. On 1st February William Watman, a gunner's mate, died of a paralytic stroke and was buried ashore. Thousands watched the Christian burial service with great respect, and followed it with their own ceremonies, which lasted three nights. A post was erected at the head of the grave, and the natives promised it would always remain.

Gradually, however, Cook and his men became aware of a change. Two shiploads of men eat a lot of food, and the natives were finding their guests expensive. Subtle hints became broad ones, and Kalaniopu and other chiefs barely hid their delight when Cook announced that the ships would sail in a day or two. They did so on 4th February, and were farewelled with every sign of affection by a vast crowd.

Cook's plan now was to complete his survey of the islands and then to sail to Kamchatka on the Asian mainland to await the summer and a final search for the north-west passage. Four days later the *Resolution*'s foremast was so badly damaged in a gale that Cook decided to return to Kealakekua Bay to have it un-stepped and repaired. It was a fatal decision.

Kalaniopu was friendly enough, but it was clear that neither he nor his people welcomed the return of the white men. Relations quickly deteriorated. A native who had been caught stealing was punished with forty lashes. A group who were helping a watering party were driven off by their priests. Friendliness gave way to insolence, and for the first time many natives went armed. On 13th February Cook, who was ashore, heard shots from the *Discovery* and saw natives in a canoe paddling hard away from the ship He assumed rightly there had been a theft of some kind, and with King, Vancouver and others he ran around the bay to intercept the canoe. He was too late, however, and natives who had so recently worshipped him now mocked and laughed at him. Without authority Thomas Edgar, master of the *Discovery*, and others tried to seize the canoe. They were stoned by an angry crowd and saved only by the intervention of Palea. Cook was angry, and according to King he was heard that night to say that the only way to put the natives in their place was to use force against them.

Early next morning it was found that the *Discovery*'s large cutter had been stolen from her mooring. Cook at once sent boats to various strategic points to prevent any canoes from leaving the bay. Then he went ashore taking a pinnace, a launch and a small cutter, with most of his marines under arms. He landed at Kavarua, and while

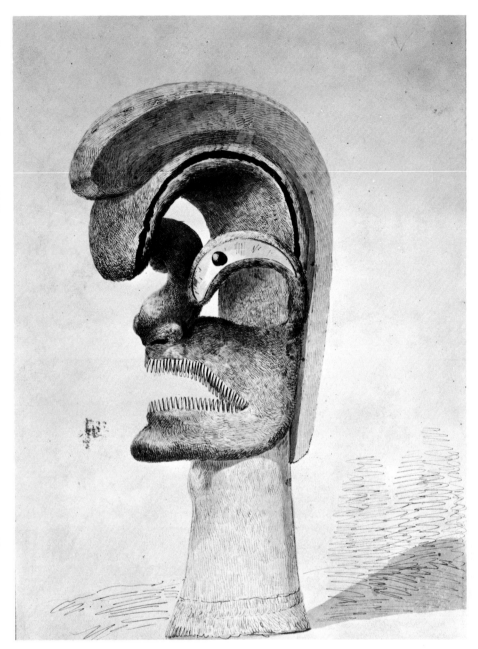

Left A view by John Webber of Nootka Sound, Vancouver Island, British Columbia, with natives and a canoe

Above Hawaiian figure with crested helmet and moveable arms.

Right A drawing by Webber of a crested, feather-covered head of the Hawaiian war god, Ku

Below An Eskimo of Unalaska, wearing a visor for protection against snow glare. By Webber

Bottom right A decorated hat from Unalaska, Aleutian Islands, of the type worn by the natives at the time of Cook's visit during his third voyage

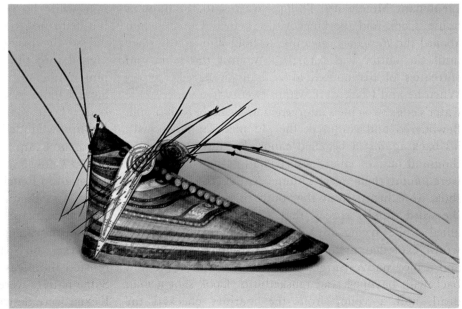

Left Hawaiians dancing for Cook and his men. They wear dog-tooth leg ornaments and carry feather shields. An unfinished drawing by Webber

Bottom left Hawaiians making a ceremonial presentation of a pig to Cook. By Webber

Right William Bligh's chart of the Hawaiian Islands, showing the tracks of the ships on their two visits, with a sketch of Kealakakua Bay, re-drawn by Henry Roberts from Bligh's survey. The point at lower left is Kavarua, where Cook was killed

Centre right Webber's drawing of Kavarua Point, on which Cook met his death

Bottom right The death of Cook by Webber. Cook was murdered at Kealakakua Bay, Hawaii, on 14th February 1779

the boats stayed offshore he and ten marines, including Lieutenant Molesworth Phillips, walked to Kalaniopu's house. Cook told the king of the theft and invited him aboard the *Resolution*, meaning to hold him as a hostage until the cutter was returned. Against the tears and entreaties of his household Kalaniopu agreed to go. When he and Cook were within twenty-five yards of the water's edge two chiefs intervened to dissuade Kalaniopu. Bewildered and confused, the old man sat down with his back against a beached canoe. By now at least two thousand natives, many armed, had gathered and more were joining them every minute. As the crowd increased shots were heard from the south side of the bay, and the word rapidly spread that a young chief had been killed while trying to launch a canoe. The natives' wrath exploded in angry shouts. Stones were thrown and armed natives surged forward. The marines fought back with bayonets and musketbutts. Cook shot a man dead, and a volley from the marines checked the

attackers momentarily. So great was their awe of Cook that while he faced them they dared not harm him. But he turned to signal the boats to come closer, and as he did so the priest Koa felled him with a club. As he sagged into the shallow water another native stabbed him in the neck and within seconds dozens, eager to have a hand in the killing, drove their daggers into his body. Four marines were killed and three, including Phillips, wounded before they managed to get away.

So, at 8 am on Sunday, 14th February 1779, died James Cook, sacrificed by the priests of Hawaii. They had made a living god of him and had then realized their error, and their only way to prove him mortal in the sight of the people was to kill him. Many great men have died for the same reason.

Clerke, on whom the command now devolved, resisted the pleas of his shipmates for massive reprisals. Some natives were killed, some canoes and the village of Kekua were destroyed and that was all. Six days later a

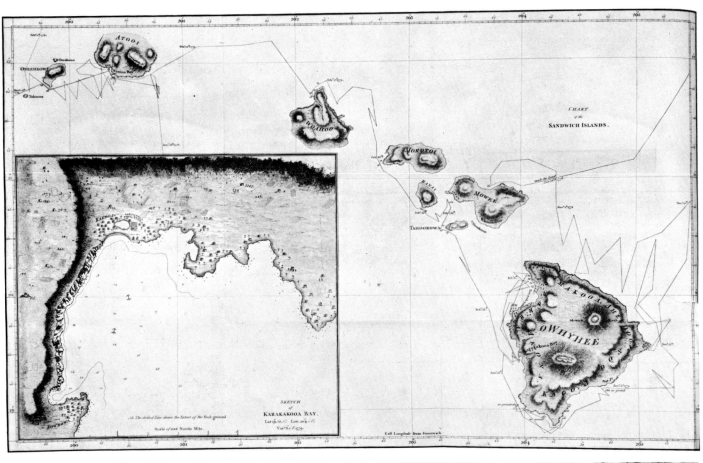

Far left This early 19th century Rockingham figure of Cook is based on the portrait by Nathaniel Dance

Left A plaque of Cook by Josiah Wedgwood

Below In French eyes Jean-François Galaup, Comte de La Pérouse, was almost as great a hero as Cook. This decorative tableau portrays in romantic style the natives of various places which the two explorers visited

Right A drawing by Ellis of two birds of Nootka Sound—the Varied Thrush (*Ixoreus naevius*) and American Robin (*Turdus migratorius*)

penitent priest handed over all that could be found of Cook's remains—his skull, leg and arm bones and hands —and as minute guns boomed out these were committed to the deep he had known and loved so well.

Clerke moved to the *Resolution* with King as his first lieutenant and Gore took over the *Discovery*. Clerke would have been well justified in returning at once to England, but instead he resolved to fulfil Cook's own plans, and so virtually signed his own death warrant for he well knew that he could never survive another season in the Arctic.

The ships sailed from Kealakekua Bay on 23rd February, and three weeks were spent completing the survey of the islands.

Kamchatka was reached in late April and the ships moored off St Peter and St Paul (Petropavlovsk). Six weeks later they sailed towards Bering Strait and the icy wastes that had beaten Cook a year earlier. Inevitably they were beaten too. On 22nd August,

two days out from Petropavlovsk on their way back Clerke died. He was buried ashore. Gore now returned to the *Resolution* as commander and King took over the *Discovery*. The long voyage home was by way of China, the East Indies and the Cape of Good Hope.

Nearing England violent winds drove both ships round the north of Scotland, and they anchored in Stromness, Orkney Islands, on 22nd August 1780. Here, almost within sight of home, died Samuel Gibson, sergeant of marines, Cook's companion on three voyages, who had once dreamed of being a king in Tahiti. King travelled ahead to London with the journals and charts of the voyage for the Admiralty. For a month the ships stayed weatherbound at Stromness, and it was 4th October when they finally anchored at The Nore. The voyage had taken four years and almost three months. In that time seven men had died from sickness (but none from scurvy), three by accident and five by violence on that fateful morning in Kealakekua Bay.

Detail from the memorial to Cook
erected by Sir Hugh Palliser at Vache
Park, Buckinghamshire

EPILOGUE

TO THE MEMORY OF
CAPTAIN JAMES COOK.

The ablest and most renowned Navigator this or any country hath produced.

He raised himself, solely by his merit from a very obscure birth, to the rank of Post Captain in the royal navy, and was, unfortunately killed by the Savages of the island Owhyhee, on the 14th of February 1779: which island he had not long before discovered, when prosecuting his third voyage round the globe.

He possessed, in an eminent degree, all the qualifications requisite for his profession and great undertakings: together with the amiable and worthy qualities of the best men. Cool and deliberate in judging: sagacious in determining: active in executing: steady and persevering in enterprising from vigilance and unremitting caution: unsubdued by labour, difficulties, and disappointments fertile in expedients: never wanting presence of mind: always possessing himself and the full use of a sound understanding:

The first news of Cook's death had reached England about nine months before the return of the expedition. It came in a letter from Clerke to Phillip Stephens sent from Petropavlovsk and received on 10th January 1780, and was published next day in the *London Gazette*. The Empress of Russia was one of the first of many crowned heads of Europe to send condolences. Most newspapers published glowing articles in praise of Cook and his achievements, and the few derogators who can always be relied upon to rush into print were sharply silenced.

The accounts of the first and second voyages had already gone into several editions and the demand for them was unabating. By order of the Admiralty an account of the third voyage was now prepared for publication, partly from Cook's own journal and partly from King's, with engravings after drawings by Webber. Half the profits from the sale of this went to Cook's widow, who also received a generous royalty from the account of the second voyage and from the sale of plates for both. Owing to the inadequacy of the copyright laws she received nothing for the many pirated editions and translations; otherwise she would have become a very wealthy woman.

At his own expense Sir Hugh Palliser erected a handsome and moving memorial to Cook on his estate at Vache Park, Chalfont St Giles, Buckinghamshire. Since then statues, memorials and obelisks have proliferated where Cook had been—from the bleak coast of Newfoundland to Point Venus, Tahiti; from the Yorkshire moors to Queen Charlotte's Sound, New Zealand. At a rough count there are known today to be about two hundred. Oddly enough perhaps the best-known is also one of the most recent—the bronze statue by Sir T. Brock, RA, which was erected in 1914 in The Mall, near Admiralty Arch and within sight of the statue of that other famous seaman, Horatio Nelson.

In Hawaii Cook's memory was held in the greatest veneration until about 1850. Then a strange change occurred. An American missionary, the Rev. Sheldon Dibble, who was almost pathologically anti-British, decided that it was necessary for the souls of the Hawaiians to blacken the memory of the man whom their ancestors had deified. Without scruple he distorted facts, taught young Hawaiian pastors and teachers to revile Cook's memory, and published his distortions as history. These were accepted and perpetuated by other writers until Cook was detested not only by all Hawaiians but by many Americans as well. It was not until this century that a scholarly investigation revealed what Dibble had done and rehabilitated Cook's good name. Today in the islands there are several memorials to Cook, and a submerged plate on the actual spot where he was killed has made Kavarua a place of pilgrimage.

Immediately King George III learned of Cook's death he granted his widow an annual pension of £250, with £25 a year each for her three sons. The loss of her husband was only one of several blows Mrs Cook was to suffer in the following years. Her second son Nathaniel, aged sixteen, was drowned in October 1780 when his ship, the *Thunderer*,

went down in a hurricane in the West Indies; her youngest son, Hugh, who was a student at Christ's College, Cambridge, died in December 1793 at the age of seventeen; and barely a month later, on 25th January 1794, her eldest and only surviving son James, aged thirty, already a commander in the Navy, was drowned off Poole while on the way to join his ship, the *Spitfire*. During her late years Mrs Cook lived chiefly with her cousin Isaac Smith at Clapham—'a handsome, venerable lady,' so a friend wrote, 'always dressed in black satin'. She died, aged ninety-three, on 13th May 1835, and was buried with her sons James and Hugh in the church of Great St Andrew's, Cambridge. To the regret of historians she had apparently destroyed all personal letters from Cook, considering them too sacred for other eyes.

The first biography of Cook was written by the Rev. Dr Andrew Kippis and appeared in 1788. Despite inaccuracies it remains a valuable work, for the author had the advantage of personal contact with Mrs Cook and men such as Sandwich, Banks, Palliser and Stephens who had known him well. Since then there have been innumerable biographical studies, but in few does the complex personality of Cook emerge with any clarity, and the definitive biography is yet to appear. However, since 1955 scholarship has been immeasurably enriched by the publication in full of Cook's journals by the Hakluyt Society, superbly edited and annotated by Dr J. C. Beaglehole, the foremost authority on Cook and the south Pacific.

Of the many tributes to Cook by those who sailed with him perhaps the one which got nearest to his real character was that written by David Samwell, who was surgeon's mate aboard the *Resolution* on the third voyage.

'Nature had endowed him with a mind vigorous and

comprehensive, which in his riper years he had cultivated with care and industry,' Samwell wrote. 'His general knowledge was extensive and various; in that of his own profession he was unequalled. With a clear judgment, strong masculine sense, and the most determined resolution; with a genius peculiarly turned for enterprise, he pursued his object with unshaken perseverance —vigilant and active in an eminent degree; cool and intrepid among dangers; patient and firm under difficulties and distress; fertile in expedients; great and original in all his designs; active and resolved in carrying them into execution. In every situation he stood unrivalled and alone; on him all eyes were turned; he was our leading-star, which at its setting left us involved in darkness and despair.

'His constitution was strong, his mode of living temperate. He had no repugnance to good living, however. He always kept a good table, though he could bear the reverse without murmuring. He was a modest man and rather bashful; of an agreeable lively conversation, sensible and intelligent. In his temper he was somewhat hasty, but of a disposition the most friendly, benevolent and humane. His person was above six feet high, and though a good-looking man he was plain both in address and appearance. His head was small, his hair, which was a dark brown, he wore tied behind. His face was full of expression, his nose exceedingly well-shaped, his eyes, which were small and of a brown cast, were quick and piercing; his eyebrows prominent, which gave his countenance altogether an air of austerity.

'He was beloved by his people, who looked up to him as to a father and obeyed his commands with alacrity. The confidence we placed in him was unremitting, our admiration of his great talents unbounded, our esteem for his good qualities affectionate and sincere.'

Top left The apotheosis of Cook. Neptune raises him to Immortality, Genius crowns him with a wreath, and Fame introduces him to history. Below Britannia is receiving tribute from the various peoples of the world

Left One of Melbourne's most prized historical assets, Captain Cook's cottage was built at Great Ayton, Yorkshire, in 1775 by his parents. The cottage was removed to its present site as a gift to the people of Victoria by Mr Russell Grimwade of Melbourne in 1934

Top right A portrait by an unknown artist of Elizabeth Cook, 'a venerable old lady in black satin'

Right A rare engraved portrait of Cook from an original by an Italian artist, Giovanni Chisor

Gio. Chisor Ad vivum pinx   *Apud Theodorum Viero Venetus*

Il Cap.º Giacomo Cook   Le Cap.ⁿ Jacques Cook
Membro della Reale Società di Londra , e   Membre de la Société Royale de Londres, et
rinomat.ᵐᵉ per li suoi Viaggi e scoperte .   très rennommé pour les Voyages, et les decouvertes

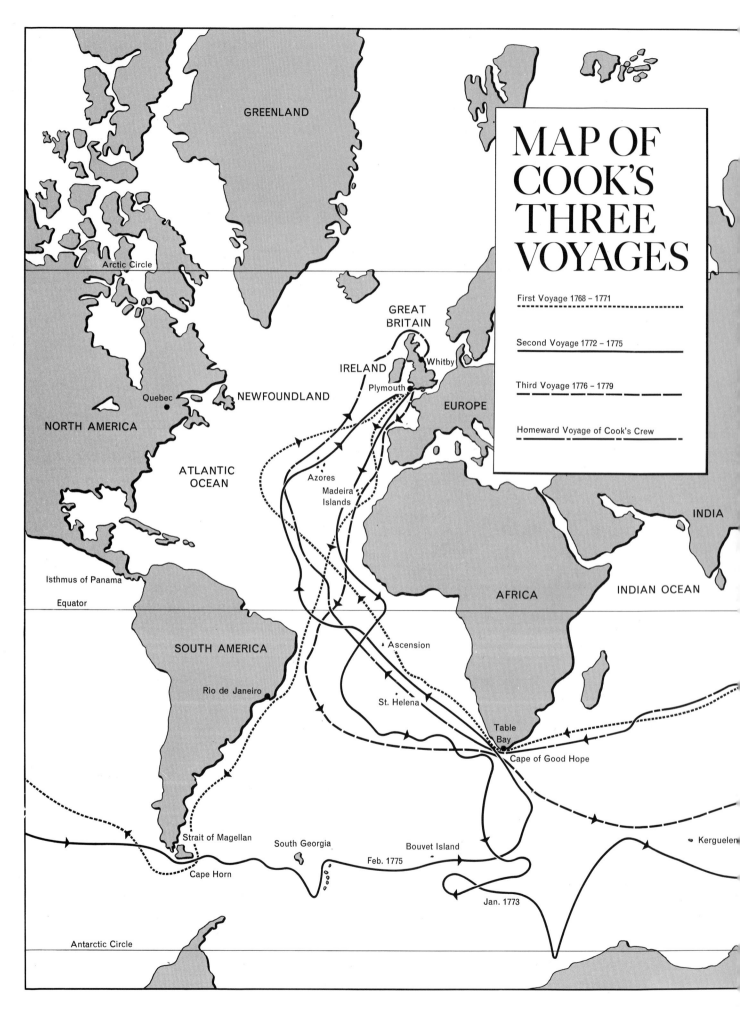

MAP OF COOK'S THREE VOYAGES

First Voyage 1768 – 1771

Second Voyage 1772 – 1775

Third Voyage 1776 – 1779

Homeward Voyage of Cook's Crew

GREENLAND

Arctic Circle

GREAT BRITAIN

IRELAND

Whitby

Plymouth

NORTH AMERICA

Quebec

NEWFOUNDLAND

EUROPE

ATLANTIC OCEAN

Azores

Madeira Islands

INDIA

Isthmus of Panama

Equator

AFRICA

INDIAN OCEAN

SOUTH AMERICA

Ascension

Rio de Janeiro

St. Helena

Table Bay

Cape of Good Hope

Kerguelen

Strait of Magellan

South Georgia

Bouvet Island

Feb. 1775

Cape Horn

Jan. 1773

Antarctic Circle

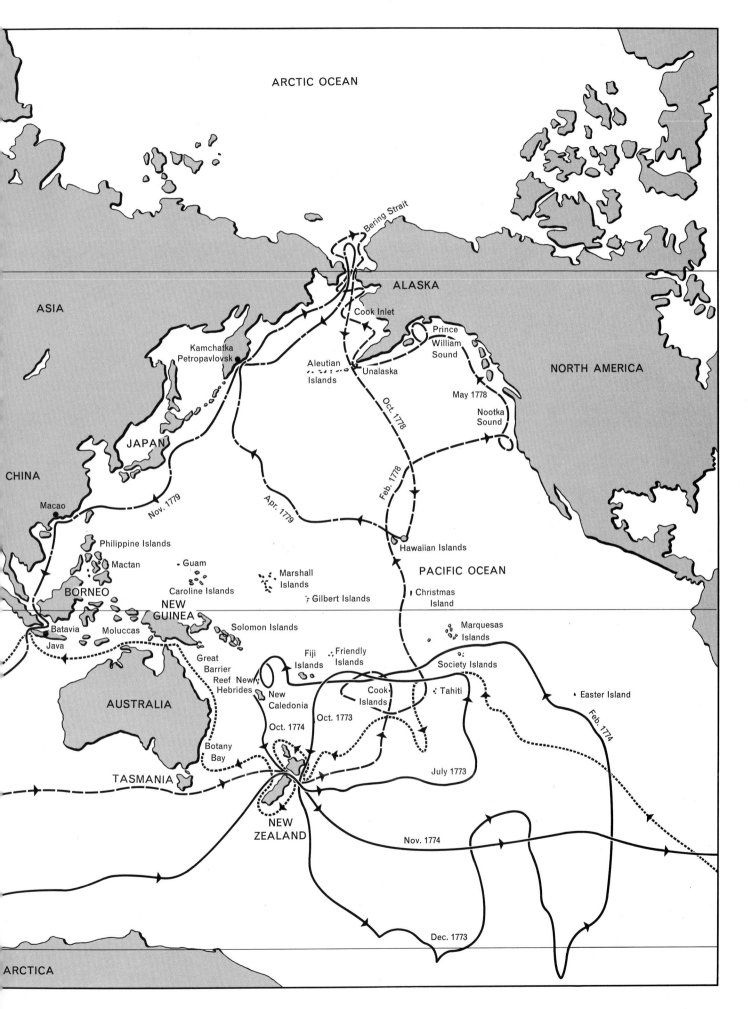

ARCTIC OCEAN

ASIA

ALASKA

Cook Inlet

Kamchatka
Petropavlovsk

Prince
William
Sound

NORTH AMERICA

Aleutian
Islands

Unalaska

May 1778

Oct. 1778

Nootka
Sound

JAPAN

CHINA

Feb. 1778

Macao

Nov. 1779

Apr. 1779

Philippine Islands

Hawaiian Islands

PACIFIC OCEAN

Mactan

Guam

Marshall
Islands

Christmas
Island

Caroline Islands

Gilbert Islands

BORNEO

NEW
GUINEA

Solomon Islands

Marquesas
Islands

Batavia

Moluccas

Java

Great
Barrier
Reef New
Hebrides

Fiji
Islands

Friendly
Islands

Society Islands

Easter Island

New
Caledonia

Cook
Islands

Tahiti

Feb. 1774

AUSTRALIA

Oct. 1774

Oct. 1773

July 1773

Botany
Bay

TASMANIA

New
Zealand

NEW
ZEALAND

Nov. 1774

Dec. 1773

ARCTICA

Bering Strait

153

INDEX

ACKNOWLEDGMENTS

The following pictures are reproduced by kind permission of:

The Admiralty Board Defence Council, London 90, 91, 101t.

Australian News & Information Bureau, London 53tr, 150t.

Berne Historical Museum 112, 114l, 122br, 152b, 127bl.

Bernice P. Bishop Museum, Honolulu 121b, 123, 142t, 142b.

The Rt Hon The Earl of Birkenhead, Banbury. Photographed by Blinckhorn photographers, Banbury 81t.

The Trustees of the British Museum, London 6, 12, *19tl*, 20, 21t, 24, 28, *30b*, *31*, 33, 34, 35l, 35r, 36, 37t, 37b, 40–1, 42, 43, 45, 46, 47, 51, 53b, 56–7, 58l, 58r, 62, *65t*, 66t, 66bl, 66br, 67l, 67r, *68t*, *80t*, 96b, 100b, 101b, 116tl, 116tr, 119tr, 121t, 122t, 122bl, 122cr, 128, *132b*, *133b*, *140*, 141tr, 143t, 143c, 151b. Photographed by Michael Holford *30t*, 48, 49, 59, 63, *69*, 105, 108l, 135t, 145. Photographed by Axel Poignant 38, 39, 54, 60, 64, 92, 96t, 104t, 104bl, 108r, 109c, 118, 119l, 126b, 138, 139, 141tl.

Dixson Galleries, Sydney by permission of the Trustees of the Public Library of New South Wales. Photographed by Brian Bird, Sydney 84, 85.

Mrs W. P. Keith, London, photographed by Axel Poignant *65b*.

Mitchell Library, Sydney. Photographed by Brian Bird, Sydney 86, 87, 100t, 109b, 143b, 148, 151t.

Museum of the American Indian, New York 141br.

Museum für Völkerkunde, Vienna 104br.

National Art Gallery, Wellington *18*.

National Gallery of Victoria *86b*.

Collection of the National Library of Australia, Canberra 94, 95, 115t, 119cr, 119br, 124t, 131, *133t*. Nan Kivell Collection of the National Library of Australia, Canberra *22–3*.

National Maritime Museum, Greenwich 16, 17t, 19b, 32, *80b*, 83t, 83c, 82–3, 88–9, *99t*, *99b*, 102–3, 106–7, 109t, 114r, 120t, *129*, 130, *132t*, 136, 137. Photographed by Michael Holford 7b, 27, 76, 77, 78, 93, *98t*, *98b*, 115b.

National Museum of Ethnology, Lieden 120b.

National Portrait Gallery, London 71.

National Publicity Studios, Wellington 81br.

The High Commissioner for New Zealand, Wellington 44, 50, 52, 53tl, 147, 157.

The Peabody Museum of Archaeology and Ethnology, Harvard University 124b, 125t, 126t, 127t, 127br, 141bl.

The Hon Mrs Clive Pearson, Parham Park, Pulborough, Sussex. Photographed by Michael Holford 26.

Philadelphia Museum of Art 134–5b.

Axel Poignant, London 19tr.

The Public Archives of Canada, Ottawa 97r, 116b.

Mr and Mrs Rex Rienits Collection, London 29, 61. Photographed by Michael Holford 55, *110–11*, 117, *144tl*, *144tr*, *144b*, 150b.

Royal Academy of Arts, London 74, 81bl.

Vic Stacey, London 5.

Whitby Literary and Philosophical Society. Photographed by Axel Poignant 10–11, 14, 15, 21b, 79. Photographed by Tindale's, Whitby 82l.

Yale University Art Gallery, gift of the Associates 97l.

Sir Hugh Palliser, who first recognised Cook's genius and became his greatest admirer, erected this monument to him at Vache Park, Buckinghamshire. It still stands and attracts many tourists